STATIONS WEST

Taken in 1867 by Carlton E. Watkins of San Francisco, this represents one of the earliest railroad scenes photographed in Oregon. To reach eastern Oregon before the coming of the Oregon Railway & Navigation Co., one boarded a riverboat in Portland and journeyed up the Columbia River to the Cascades. From there the traveler rode the small portage railroad several miles around the most troublesome part of the river. This photograph shows connection being made from the railroad to the riverboat Oneonta for a continuation of the trip up the river.

What is missing from this scene? The railroad station, but this luxury was yet to come to the West

STATIONS WEST

By

EDWIN D. CULP

The CAXTON PRINTERS, Ltd.
Caldwell, Idaho
1972

International Standard Book Number 0-87004-219-X

Library of Congress Catalog Card No. 70-150814

Lithographed and bound in the United States of America by
The CAXTON PRINTERS, Ltd.
Caldwell, Idaho   83605
115851

To the memory of my father, Edward Alexander Culp, a railroad train conductor in Oregon for over fifty years, who began on the Sumpter Valley at Baker in 1899, joined the Oregon Railway & Navigation Co. in 1900, and came to the Southern Pacific in 1912.

And to the memories of my paternal and maternal grandfathers, both of whom helped build the ORN in this state.

Edward A. Culp in his caboose

"Of all there was I now recall
That made my boy heart glad,
I wish that I might go again
Over the line with Dad."
—Anonymous

TABLE OF CONTENTS

Preface *page* ix

Introduction 3

1. Portland Railroad Yards 7
   Union Station, Portland 9

2. The Oregon & California Railroad Company;
   Portland to Eugene (SP) 11

3. The Oregon & California Railroad Company;
   Eugene to Ashland (SP) 30

4. The Oregon & California Railroad Company;
   Westside Division (SP) 39

5. The Oregon Railway & Navigation Company (UP) 43

6. The Joseph Branch (OR&N-UP) 60
   The Heppner Branch (OR&N-UP) 62

7. The Northern Pacific Railway (BN) 63

8. Narrow Gauge Rail Lines in the Willamette Valley (SP) 65
   Dayton, Sheridan & Grand Ronde Railroad Company 65
   The Oregonian Railway Company, Limited 65
   Portland and Willamette Valley Railway Company 69

9. The Oregon Pacific Railroad (SP) 82

10. The Sumpter Valley Railway Company 91

11. Malheur Valley Railway Company (UP) 96
    Ilwaco Railway & Steam Navigation Company Railroad (UP) 98
    The Columbia Southern Railway (UP) 100
    The Great Southern Railroad 103
    The Oregon Short Line (UP) 104
    Mount Hood Railroad Co. (UP) 105

12. Pacific Railway & Navigation Company (SP) 106

13. The Astoria-Seaside Line (BN) 115
    The Portland & Southwestern Railroad 122

14. The Oregon Trunk Railway (BN) 123
    The Des Chutes Railroad (UP) 123

15. The City of Prineville Railroad 128
    Pacific & Eastern Railway Company (SPS) 132

16. The Albany and Lebanon Railroad (SP) 133
    Beaverton & Willsburg Railroad Company (SP) 134

17. Coos Bay, Roseburg & Eastern Railroad and Navigation
    Company (SP) 136

18. California & Northeastern Railroad (SP) 142
    Nevada-California-Oregon Railway (SP) 148

19. Corvallis & Alsea River Railway Company (SP) 148
    Portland & Oregon City Railway Company 150

20. Oregon & Southeastern Railway Company 151
    Willamina & Grand Ronde Railway Company 154
    Oregon, California & Eastern Railway (BN-SP) 161

21. Salem, Falls City & Western Railway Company (SP) 163

22. Rogue River Valley Railroad Company 169
    Valley & Siletz Railroad 172

23. The Willamette Bridge Railway Company 178
    The Portland & Vancouver Railway 179

24. The East Side Railway Company 182

25. Willamette Valley Southern Railway Company 195

26. The Oregon Electric Railway (BN) 198

27. United Railway Company (BN) 216
    Walla Walla Valley Traction Co. (BN) 220

28. Portland, Eugene & Eastern Railway (SP) 222
    The Red Electrics (SP) 230

29. Short Rail Lines in Oregon 248

30. Trolley Park and Washington Park Station 254

    Index 260

Abbreviations:
    (BN) . . . Burlington Northern Inc.
    (OR&N) . . . Oregon Railway and Navigation Company
    (SP) . . . Southern Pacific Company
    (SPS) . . . Spokane Portland & Seattle RR Co.
    (UP) . . . Union Pacific Railroad Company

PREFACE

In preparing material for a book on Oregon railroads, I have to some extent disregarded the love of rail buffs for close-up views of rolling stock. An engine picture does have beauty, but a photo of a railroad station with folk arriving and departing follows the purpose of the book more closely, illustrating the full Oregon railroad scene.

The largest portion of these pictures was copied from private collections—which usually featured the collections' owners, their relatives or their close friends—and from the collections of rail fans. Some are copies of old postcards sold during the early part of the century. Edwin Cooke Patton, owner of the Patton Post Card Company of Salem and one of the many fine postcard photographers, must have been a great lover of trains, stations, and their towns because he left a rich legacy of Northwest Americana for future generations to enjoy.

The station buildings themselves, those that are still left, are fascinating to the architectural enthusiast. Edward H. Harriman, with his influence on the Oregon scene, developed the two-story structure offering living quarters for the agent upstairs. The Southern Pacific built a bungalow dwelling with an open-end undercover portion following a de-

sign used in California. James J. Hill, on the Oregon Electric lines, devised a very attractive chalet structure. All of these stations had personalities of their own.

During the late nineteenth and early twentieth centuries, Oregon life in the small village or town centered around the railroad station. Things happened there: People came and left daily, and late news flashes could be heard over the wires of the railroad telegraph. Many of the weekly newspapers had a special column in every issue advising that Mr. C—— had arrived this week or Miss P—— had departed on Train 31. People didn't care about fancy train names; they loved referring to them by their numbers.

The Oregon picture would be incomplete without the hard-working local agent who prepared the railroad tickets, checked baggage, operated the telegraph key and proudly served in the role of Mr. Railroad for his community. It always seemed a typical agent should have a green visor to protect his eyes, black arm bands for his shirt sleeves, and a heavy chain attached to his important watch. Many of his counterparts will be found in these pages.

I am most grateful for the helpful assistance given so willingly by Jack C.

Murray, publisher's representative for
The Caxton Printers, Ltd., who helped
me get this book in order. Some of those
who have offered suggestions, loaned
pictures, and supplied information are:
Henry Ortez of the Southern Pacific,
George J. Skorney of the Union Pacific,
and Walter Grande and Vern Vasey of
the Burlington Northern; Betty Book,
Alden Moberg, and Margaret Keiller of
the Oregon State Library, along with
Hugh Morrow of the Salem City Library
(where I was permitted the use of
the Ben Maxwell Collection); Harriet
Moore and Sally Wilson of the State
University archives; Priscilla Knuth of
the Oregon Historical Society; C. Ray
Lindsay of Rockaway; George Abdill of
Roseburg; Brooks Hawley of Baker; Wilmer Gardner of Oregon City; Alfred Haij
and John T. Labbe of Portland; Arden
Hammer of Aumsville; Clark M. Will,
Robert Wynne Wilson, Howard Mader,
Louise A. Maxwell, and Charles F. West
of Salem; and Guy Dunscomb and Harold Hinshaw respectively of Modesto
and Santa Clara, California.

STATIONS WEST

INTRODUCTION

Portland, December 7, 1887

To The Editor of the OREGONIAN:

I am extremely desirous of saying something that may attract the attention of our state railroad commissioners to the condition of the narrow gauge railroad running from Portland to Coburg via Woodburn. I have just arrived here from Macleay, after an unwarrantable exposure of life and limb to the dangers of utter annihilation, or the more probable certainty of physical dissolution from old age; and a due regard for the safety of the next generation demands that suitable warning be given by one who has been through the mill and is able to speak as a probable sole survivor.

Yesterday morning I walked from my farm to Macleay, a distance of two miles, through one of the worst wind and rain storms that ever visited this country. During the walk I had used a heavy overcoat and a pair of gum boots, which I left at the depot. I had no sooner entered the car than I discovered my mistake; there was where I most needed those articles of protection from the angry elements, but they were left, and so was I.

After I uncovered the Conductor, who was buried under a pile of remnants of waterproof, and "brought him to" to a degree that he could receive my fare, I turned my attention to the discovery of some location where I could safely anchor in the rising flood.

There was but one seat in the entire car that had not a puddle of water on the cushion, and upon that I ventured to squat, and proceeded to read THE OREGONIAN I had obtained at the station. Just as I had become deeply interested in the troubles of the French Cabinet, and wondered who would be the next president, I suddenly felt a coolness manifested between myself and the seat, which seemed to demand immediate investigation. A vigilant exploration disclosed the alarming fact that I was just entering on the incipient stages of an impromptu "sitz" bath.

Now, I never did like to take a "sitz" bath with my clothes on; in fact, while I can stand wet feet and wet arms and shoulders with a noticeable degree of equanimity, whenever the water begins to run under that part of my anatomical formation commonly employed for purposes of rest while in a sitting posture, I get "riled." But I still held my peace.

At Silverton the locomotive left the train at the depot and went up town and was gone nearly a half hour.[1] Sensible locomotive! In the meantime, however, the storm became more furious and the passengers were compelled to get on the inside in order to escape its blinding violence. The floor and the seats were the only part of the car that didn't leak, and they held all they got with a tenacity of purpose that suggest the nature of their average owner.

At Woodburn, Mr. Scott, the receiver of the road, got aboard, or rather afloat, and it was a source of great consolation to see that after pulling his coat off on entering the car, he put it on again in less than five minutes as the only available substitute for a life preserver. It brought the very moisture to our—feet to see the solicitude with which he went through the car and set the cushions on end against the windows for purposes of drainage. It was noticeable that he didn't sit down; he seemed to be troubled and undecided as to what to do; in fact, he seemed to be "on a stand," and so deeply did he enlist the sympathy of the passengers that they all joined him.

A few miles this side of Woodburn the train stopped as suddenly as it is possible for a slow train to stop, and a Brakeman went back a hundred yards and picked up an old battered tin bucket, and we waited until he returned. The Manager remarked to me that he presumed

the bucket blew off the platform; but why they should stop to recover a 5-cent bucket was a mystery to me until I reflected that it might be the only utensil on board that could be used for bailing purposes. It was that old bucket or death, and, as far as I could see, it was likely to be both.

We crossed the river at Ray's Landing[2] on the Margey,[3] a boat whose name was the only attractive thing about it: There was not a dry board or a seat anywhere to be found, and still we were "on the stand." A train of cars was waiting for us on this side of the river, but the locomotive had gone to Dundee to fire up,[4] so we fired up too, but it didn't do any good. As soon as we arrived, a man was sent afoot across the woods to notify the engineer that we had come, and were ready to receive any communication he might deem it proper to make.

In less than an hour he arrived, and we were again on the road—that is, they claimed we were, but I will never know. It was dark by this time, and if we were on any "road" it must have been some

---

[1] There was a spur track serving a grain elevator about a half-mile uptown from the main line track (about where the Silverton police station is today). The train was probably a Mixed, meaning that some freight cars as well as passenger cars were carried.

[2] For some time a riverboat left Portland in the morning and plied its way up the Willamette River to discharge its passengers at Ray's Landing for connections with the ORR for Silverton, Macleay and Coburg; and at Fulquartz Landing for a rail trip to Sheridan and Dallas. (Ray's Landing was on the east side of the river, Fulquartz on the west.) After the Portland and Willamette Valley Railway extension had been completed from Dundee to Portland, water service was discontinued.

[3] The Margey was the boat used to transport passengers across the river. A bridge was started here but was never completed.

[4] This was the headquarters and roundhouse for the line. The engine was either undergoing repairs or refueling. Dundee is a half-mile from the landing.

timber road running out to the Tualatin plains. This car didn't leak, the roof having been put on top instead of being used for a floor, but it is the roughest railroad on the face of the earth.

I had started to Portland to consult Drs. Darrin as to the best treatment of a disordered liver, but before we had reached Dundee my liver was well. It was necessary to continue the journey, however, to readjust a spinal column arbitrarily shortened four inches, and to extricate a shoulder blade from a suffering windpipe.

At this point in my journey, my patience gave out and I concluded to speak of the matter in THE OREGONIAN, and actually commenced this letter there, but since I couldn't keep my hat on, how could I write? I rapidly changed my communication into my will, and began conversing with a gentleman in the same seat with myself, but every time I would speak the car would give a sudden lurch, and my remark would be delivered in the ear of a lady sitting in the seat across the aisle.

These lurches became so common that I found it necessary to anticipate them, and when they would fail to come of course the remark would go across the aisle all the same. The lurch would sometimes "go to grass," but the remark always got there smiling. This is the result of a force of habit that is justly attributable to the outrageous condition of the road, and there the blame must be fixed.

We came to a washout about six miles from Portland and waited an hour for a boat that came an hour afterwards and landed us here at 7 o'clock. We left Macleay before 11 and arrived in Portland eight hours afterwards. Fifty miles in eight hours. Six miles an hour accounts for the fact that no accidents ever occur on this road.

It is no uncommon thing for a locomotive and a train of cars to be ditched on this road. Not long since a locomotive fell off the track near Macleay and lay on its side and bellowed and screeched like a wounded sheik of the illimitable desert, until the neighboring farmers came with rails and crowbars and put it on its legs again. A short time ago the train that was due at Macleay at 2 P.M. didn't arrive until 12 that night. The whole business got off the track twice somewhere in the woods.

It changes its "schedule time" every few months, but that never makes any difference in the arrival or departure of trains.

The only way to catch a train on this road is to go with your blankets and a basket of grub and wait for the whistle; and you never want to buy a limited ticket, for if it doesn't expire before you get there, you will.

Upon arrival at Ray's landing the hands walk back two miles[5] for supper, bed and breakfast, and return next morning, on foot.

_____
[5] This would have been to St. Paul, a small nearby town.

This road runs through a good country, and its employes are clever and careful. Mr. Scott, the receiver, seems to be doing all in his power to keep it going, but in the unfortunate legal difficulties which surround it we can see the cause of its present condition.

Something, however, ought to be done to insure greater safety and comfort to passengers, and the state railroad commissioners ought to come to Macleay on some rainy day and learn from sad experience.

T. T. Geer
(Reprinted from the Portland ORE-
GONIAN, December 11, 1887)

The writer, Theodore Thurston Geer, was the tenth governor of Oregon, serving from 1899 to 1903. He lived, then, on a farm near Macleay in Marion County. The letter was written shortly before the line was taken over by the Oregon & California Railroad. (The line was even later acquired by the Southern Pacific).

A railroad station on the Oregon Railroad named after Governor Geer

CHAPTER 1

PORTLAND RAILROAD YARDS, 1885

The Oregon & California Railroad station was located at Front and Flanders Streets (right front) and the Northern Pacific Railroad station was a block away, at Front and Glisan Streets (left center). Today, Union Station is located at Hoyt/Irving Streets, the next two blocks over (Portland's streets run alphabetically in this area). Because it was located at the Ash Street Wharf, the Oregon Railway & Navigation Company's station cannot be seen.

Looking northward, this etching shows the railroad center of Portland in 1885, before the Union Station was constructed and before the first railroad bridge across the Willamette River was opened.

Today, Couch Lake (top left) is a fill and is the present location of Union Station. The Willamette is on the right.

The NP train is heading north for St. Helens, Columbia City, and Goble. At Goble, a connection was made with a ferry which took the entire train—engine included—across the river to Kalama, Washington, and thence on to Tacoma.

The train moving south on the trestle was an O&C, soon to start up Fourth Street in Portland for Beaverton and Hillsboro. Passengers enroute to Oregon City and Salem would board the O&C ferry (not shown) at the foot of

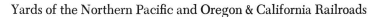

Yards of the Northern Pacific and Oregon & California Railroads

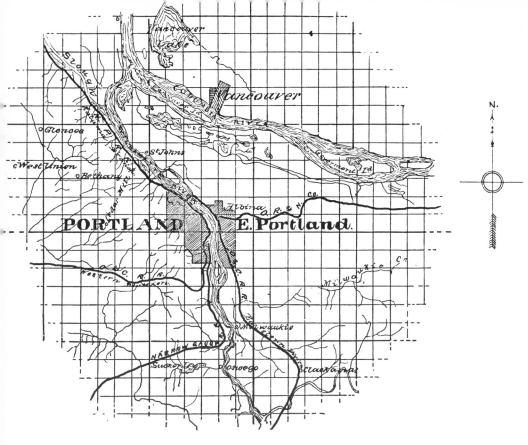

PORTLAND, OREGON.

Map of Portland of the late '80s showing the routes of trains entering the city.

Union Station under construction, June, 1894. High water has temporarily halted the building program.

Union Station at the foot of Sixth Street in Portland as it looked in the early years of this century. Note the hotel busses waiting to serve the traveling public.

Flanders Street, cross the Willamette to Holladay Avenue on the East Side, and board the train in East Portland.

UNION STATION, PORTLAND
(BN–SP–UP)

Portland's Union Station was built in 1893-94 as a part of the Northern Pacific Terminal Company. The NPT Co. was set up by Henry Villard in the '80s as a separate organization to function as a station facility in Portland for all incoming and outgoing trains.

Van Brunt & Howe of Boston were the architects for the Union Station. Henry Van Brunt had successfully constructed many other well known stations throughout the United States, including ones for Ogden, Omaha, and Cheyenne.

The station reached its maximum ca-

Union Depot News Stand, Portland, Oregon.

The interior of Union Station taken about 1910, showing the newsstand. Today this section of the building is used for the ticket office. Note the hard seats with metal dividers and the cuspidor for the gentleman's convenience.

pacity on September 10, 1922, when the Spokane, Portland & Seattle Railroad started operating all of its trains from the Union Station. This made a total of ninety trains daily, fifty-two steam and thirty-eight electric. A train moved in or out every eleven minutes during the seventeen-hour period between 6:30 A.M. and 11:30 P.M.

Jack Jones is the present manager of Union Station. He replaced Colonel Harry D. Mudgett shortly after the close of World War II. Some of the best known stationmasters were Joseph Lockner, James Proffitt, Sidney Jacobs, and George Slingerland. James L. Miller, who had served as ticket agent for many years, was followed by Frank M. Smith.

The NPT Co. recently changed its name to Portland Terminal Railroad Company.

CHAPTER 2

THE OREGON & CALIFORNIA RAILROAD (SP)

It was 1869 and Oregon entered the year hardly able to wait until it had a railroad. The Congress of the United States, endeavoring to encourage rail construction, passed the U.S. Federal Land Grant Act. This brought about a power struggle among different factions in Oregon to meet the terms. The Act stated that the group completing the first twenty miles of railroad from Portland southward into the Willamette Valley would be declared the winner. The prize was every other alternate section of land bordering the track. Some of this land contained large stands of timber and deposits of minerals, as well as choice farming areas. The railroad could sell these various commodities (including the land), and the profit

realized could be used to pay construction costs, buy rolling stock and pay other railroad expenses.

Two groups in Oregon jockeyed for the advantage. They were evenly matched at the outset, since neither had any money to start construction. Ben Holladay arrived in Oregon seasoned in the transportation business by years of operating stagecoach lines. His money

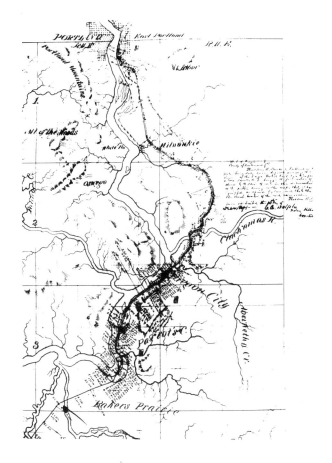

A copy of the original map submitted by the Oregon Central Railroad (Oregon & California) charting the first twenty miles of trackage built in Oregon. The completed railroad from East Portland in Multnomah County to Parrot Creek in Clackamas county. The OCR furnished a letter of attachment from President I. R. Moores, and a letter of acknowledgement from Oregon Governor George L. Woods was sent in reply. The map with these supporting documents entitled the railroad to Federal and State Land Grants as payment for its construction to California.

and know-how were the deciding factors that started the line in 1869.

Holladay, in addition to building the Oregon & California Railroad, had invested heavily in large fleets of ships operating up and down the coast and in foreign trade. Rate wars among the various steamship lines took much of his funds. In order to remain solvent and keep his ships and trains operating, he borrowed large sums of money from residents of Germany.

From Portland, Holladay contructed two separate lines, each divided by the Willamette River. The East Side Line, operating out of Portland from the east side of the river, reached Eugene October 15, 1871; Oakland July 7, 1872; and Roseburg December 3 of the same year. The West Side Line, running up Portland's Fourth Street, reached Hillsboro December 23, 1871, and St. Joseph, a town on the Yamhill River near McMinnville long since abandoned, on November 3, 1872. No further work was done on the road for more than eight years. Holladay was near bankruptcy. The financial crisis of 1873 allowed Henry Villard, who represented the German bondholders, to take over the line.

It was to be some eight years before Villard resumed construction. At last,

Ben Holladay, 1901

on May 4, 1884, the O&C reached Ashland, but shortly afterward the Villard regime crashed. The Southern Pacific secured a lease on the O&C and finished construction. A connection with their own line was made in 1887, opening through railroad service from Portland to California.

☞ *Clockwise from top left:* Map issued with O&C's first public timetable; the first public timetable, issued July, 1887, before through train service was available; a placard associated with the early days of the O&C in Oregon; an annual pass and a paycheck personally signed by Ben Holladay; a ferry check which entitled the bearer to cross the Willamette River on an O&C ferry (prior to the construction of the railroad bridge); an advertisement of the 1870s.

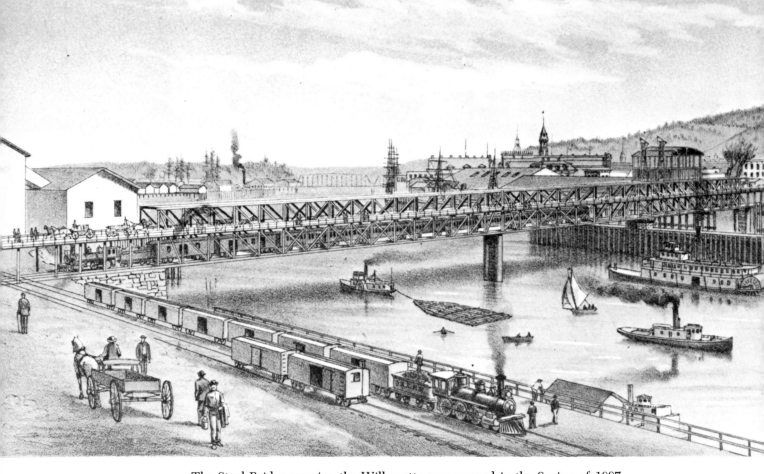

The Steel Bridge crossing the Willamette was opened in the Spring of 1887

The East Morrison Street Station, located at 3rd Avenue and S.E. Morrison Street on the east side of the Willamette in Portland, offered a big advantage to the traveling public residing in that section of the city. It was the first stop after leaving Portland's Union Station. The building was constructed of hollow cement blocks manufactured by Southern Pacific's own people in southern Oregon. Some of the last agents to serve here were Mrs. Ella Rice, M. D. Copenhaver and Vern Prodfitt. The building was dismantled in January, 1946.

The Brooklyn Shops in Portland, Oregon, 1924

Clackamas was originally called Marshville. When, in 1871, the town made application for a post office, the U.S. Government turned them down because a town of a similar name existed on the coast of Oregon. Thus, the Oregon & California Railroad cash book for December, 1871, shows Marshville on one side of the ledger and the new name, Clackamas, on the other. The photo below shows Clackamas on Sunday at 11 A.M., June 25, 1916. *Below right,* Harlan H. Messal, the present agent at Clackamas.

CHAUTAUQUA STATION (O&C–SP 1901

This notice might have been for any Chautauqua year:

The season of 1901
A continuous round of pleasure
Gladstone Park
A Paradise
For the Pleasure Seekers
A Health-Giving Resort
Where Recreation, Art, Song,
Oratory are Combined
The Programme Is Replete
With Good Things

Willamette Valley Chautauqua Association
8ᵗʰ Annual Assembly
July 3 to 13

Gladstone Park
Oregon City, Or

"Gladstone Park, situated on the Southern Pacific Railway twelve miles from Portland, and two miles from Oregon City, is a beautiful natural park thickly covered with gnarled oak and stately fir, providing delightful shade for hundreds of campers who resort annually to the park to partake of the entertainment and instruction provided by the management of the Willamette Valley Chautauqua Assn. . . ."

To Chautauqua Grounds, 1901

GLADSTONE TRAIN SERVICE
JULY 3RD TO 13TH, INCLUSIVE
In connection with City & Suburban Ry. Electric Lines

ROUND TRIP, 55 cents; from any point in Portland, including admission to Park.   Round Trip Tickets may be secured from THE CITY & SUBURBAN STREET RAILWAY Conductors.

Southern Pacific Trains

Leave Portland,				Leave Oregon City,	
"	"	Grand Central Station,	8:30 A.M.	Leave Oregon City, - - - -	7:00 A.M.
"	"	East Washington St.,	9:30 A.M.	" " " - - -	9:22 A.M.
"	"	" " "	11:30 A.M.	" " " - - -	10:30 A.M.
"	"	" " "	1:00 P.M.	" " " - - -	12:15 P.M.
"	"	" " "	2:45 P.M.	" " " - - -	1:45 P.M.
"	"	Grand Central Station,	4:00 P.M.	" " " - - -	3:40 P.M.
"	"	East Washington St.,	4:30 P.M.	" " " - - -	5:50 P.M.
"	"	" " "	6:30 P.M.	" " " - - -	6:30 P.M.
"	"	" " "	7:15 P.M.		
"	"	Grand Central Station,	8:30 P.M.		

Trains for GLADSTONE ONLY will leave Oregon City at 7:15, 7:40, 8:00, 8:30 and 9:20 every evening on the above dates.

Street Cars crossing Morrison St. Bridge connect with all Southern Pacific trains.
Trains leave Gladstone for Portland and Oregon City at 10:00 P.M.

From points on Southern Pacific lines south of Oregon City, tickets will be sold to the Chautauqua Assembly on the certificate plan—attendants paying full fare going, and one-third returning.   Receipts for fare must be taken in all cases, which the Secretary will attest.

C. H. MARKHAM,
G. P. A., Sou. Pac. Co.

H. D. WILCOX,
Sec'y W. V. C. Ass'n.

Oregon City, the first capital of the Oregon Territory, is the oldest incorporated town west of the Rocky Mountains. The photo to the left, taken in 1889, shows the Flyer operating between Roseburg and Portland.

Lv. Roseburg	6:20 A.M.
stopping Oregon City	2:59 P.M.
Ar. Portland	4:00 P.M.

Right, Separated from its earlier counterpart by nearly three-quarters of a century, this train—also northbound, stopped in Oregon City in 1961.

Candidate Benjamin Harrison's special train stopped for a ten-minute political speech in 1889. Later that year he was elected the twenty-third president of the United States.

The train crew smiled for the camera from the pilot of the engine in 1893. In the background the New Era post office and railroad station can be seen. The arrival of the Oregon & California Railroad in 1870 brought a "new era" to the people of this small community; hence, the name. The man at the far left is Mr. Wood Young, the conductor. John C. Newbury holds the hand of a small girl, now Mrs. John Thompson.

Canby was named after Major General Edward R. S. Canby, who was killed at a peace parley with the Modoc Indians in southern Oregon. This photograph shows the peaceful little hamlet as it appeared about 1910.

Archie S. Markee was the agent at Canby for thirty-five years. In addition to acting as mayor and president of the Chamber of Commerce, he financed three sons through college, and today they are all specialists in medicine.

AURORA, 1874. The O&C No. 1 Mail and Express stopped to allow passengers to eat

AURORA (O&C–SP)

In the spring of 1856, Aurora—or Aurora Mills, as it was then called—came into being, the first Christian communistic colony in the West. Here everyone worked to put all gain into a common fund, and no one was wealthy or poor. Lawsuits were unknown.

The colony was particularly famous for its fine German food. Ben Holladay, President of the Oregon & California Railroad, worked out an arrangement with Dr. Wilhelm Keil, head of the settlement, to feed train passengers from the famous cuisine.

In 1874 this advertisement for the Aurora Hotel appeared in the city directory

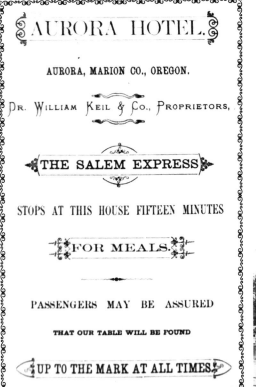

AURORA HOTEL.

AURORA, MARION CO., OREGON.

Dr. William Keil & Co., Proprietors,

THE SALEM EXPRESS

STOPS AT THIS HOUSE FIFTEEN MINUTES

FOR MEALS.

PASSENGERS MAY BE ASSURED

THAT OUR TABLE WILL BE FOUND

UP TO THE MARK AT ALL TIMES.

Below, The Aurora station in 1910

This photograph of the arrival at Woodburn of the morning train from Portland was taken in 1907

WOODBURN (SP–OE–ORR)
1915

The history of Woodburn is linked very closely with the development of the railroad. The Oregon & California Railroad Company built through here in 1870, and Jess Settlemier founded the town in 1871. In 1880 the Oregonian Railway Company, Ltd., a narrow gauge line, built from Ray's Landing on the Willamette River through St. Paul and Woodburn enroute to Silverton and Brownsville. In 1910 the Oregon Electric built a new station on their main line between Portland and Eugene at Woodburn. The OE built their right-of-way into Woodburn over the original grade between Ray's Landing and Woodburn that had long since been abandoned by the old Oregonian Railway Co.

Below, A SP Mixed (a train carrying both freight and passenger equipment) leaves the main line at Woodburn—the tracks to California—and heads out on a branch line for Mt. Angel and Silverton. An Oregon Electric car can be seen in the street.

This town, located in the heart of the French Prairie area of the Willamette Valley, was named after Joseph Gervais who came to Oregon with the Hunt party of the Astor Expedition in 1811. The photograph was taken in 1910.

Marion David Henning was the agent in Gervais for over forty years.

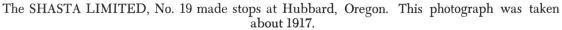

The SHASTA LIMITED, No. 19 made stops at Hubbard, Oregon. This photograph was taken about 1917.

1871: The O&C railroad station was, as the townspeople described it, "beyond the most remote suburb." The people of Salem refused to pay Ben Holladay an additional $30,000 for laying track to the center of the small town. So the track was built via the shortest north-south route. The station pictured here burned down in 1885.

1889: People continued to complain over the distance involved to reach the O&C station. The first horse-drawn street car was operated from the station to downtown Salem, a distance of one and a half miles. In 1890-91 Herbert Hoover, as a young boy dressed in uniform, worked as a conductor on both of these cars shown in the picture. Hoover's uncle, Dr. Henry J. Minthorn, was president of the Oregon Land Company, which owned the horse-drawn streetcar line. This station was dismantled shortly before World War I.

1910: The Salem railroad station with the train arriving from Portland. In the background the old state capitol building can be seen; it was destroyed by fire in 1935.

1960: The present Salem railroad station in what is today the center of town. The Shasta Daylight, shown here, left Portland at 7:45 A.M. stopped at Salem at 8:55 A.M., and arrived in San Francisco at 11:30 P.M., the fastest advertised schedule ever operated from Oregon to the Bay Area. In the background the new State Capitol can be seen.

HERBERT HOOVER

                The Waldorf-Astoria Towers
                New York 22, New York
                January 9, 1955

Dear Mr. Culp:

        At one time I was office boy
in the street car office in Salem--
also in a real estate office.

        On holidays I was dressed in
uniform and served as a conductor during
high traffic. That was about the year
1891-1892.

                Yours faithfully,

                Herbert Hoover

Mr. E. D. Culp
2790 Ellis Avenue
Salem, Oregon

A Bill of Lading signed by the agent in Salem, 1883

The interior of the Salem passenger station, October 1902. Harold A. Hinshaw, agent, is at the extreme left. Some of the other agents that served the station were W. W. Skinner, Carl Larson, and Ralph McCormick. The present agent is C. Keith Harris.

Today, these three stations in the Willamette Valley are gone, like so many other small town ticket agencies. In these towns the local passenger trains are only a memory.

Abany, Oregon, an 1899 view of the SP eating house, railroad station, and hotel, all in one building. Here SP Train No. 11, The Shasta Express, had a twenty-minute luncheon stop.

An early view of the SP eating house, Albany Oregon

A later view of the same building showing Miss Anna Wald with some of the other SP dining room waitresses in front of the building. A young engineer, James J. Kirby, often ate here and was waited on by Miss Wald. They became acquainted and she eventually became Mrs. Kirby. Some years later, James Kirby could be found in the No. 1 position on the Engineers' Seniority Roster. Their son, today, is one of the SP purchasing department officials in San Francisco.

Above left, The Albany station, constructed of hollow cement blocks, as it appeared in 1912; *right,* Paul K. Bonney, Albany's agent-operator.

The Oregon & California Railroad, in building from Portland south, projected two different routes —The East Side Line, via Oregon City and Salem, and The West Side Line, via Hillsboro and Corvallis. Both of these lines, while separating at Portland, were to meet at a point designated as Junction City—thus giving the town its name. The West Side Line reached Corvallis in 1880, and it was to be many years before any further rail building was done from here. The East Side Line built to Eugene and south, passing through Junction City, a city that never became a rail junction at all. This photograph of Junction City was taken in 1895.

The Eugene station as it looked in 1890. The beautiful park that surrounded the structure has since been replaced by parking area. Palm tree plants can always be seen in the older Eugene photographs—SP's reminder to travel California on their railroad and enjoy the palms in all their beauty.

EUGENE (O&C–SP)

The Oregon & California Railroad reached Eugene October 8, 1871—124 miles of railroad from Portland. This was a division point for the passenger trains. A Eugene newspaper of that date commented upon the arrival of the train: "Travel between Portland and Sacramento will now be 258 miles by rail and about 345 miles by stage, the connections being made at Eugene in Oregon and at Red Bluff in California. The time between railroad terminals (Eugene and Red Bluff) has been 4½ days by stage but with the setting in of the rains it is now and probably will remain through the winter at 5½ days."

The Eugene station as it looked in 1910. Note the wooden coaches with the colored glass, circle-top windows, and the many wheelmen, probably from the University of Oregon, on hand to meet incoming, or say goodbye to outgoing friends.

CHAPTER 3

This photograph of the Springfield Station taken in 1910 shows the handsome Swiss chalet type of structure that afforded living quarters for the agent.

Richard Buick, the agent at Springfield.

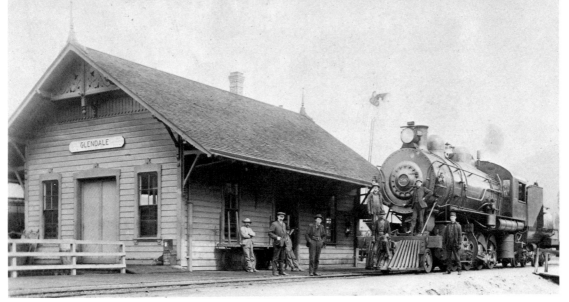

R. K. Montgomery, Glendale's agent at the time, poses with the local train crew in 1898

Stations along the line. Note the McKeen motor car at Talent

The old Roseburg station, 1890

ROSEBURG (O&C–SP)

Ben Holladay's Oregon & California Railroad reached Roseburg on December 3, 1872, where construction halted for eight years. The Panic of 1873-74 allowed Henry Villard to seize control of the line. Holladay's money, acquired by the sale of bonds in advance of construction, had been spent, and Holladay could not meet his financial obligations.

Traffic revenue from the sparsely settled region was not sufficient to meet expenses, and when bond interests could not be met, Holladay was forced out and the property and railroad was taken over by the investors. Villard continued the construction of the O&C southward from Roseburg in June 1881.

The new Roseburg station, 1915

The railroad-stage connection at Siskiyou station, 1886

THE GREAT TRAIN ROBBERY

The most infamous train robbery in Oregon's history took place at the entrance to Tunnel No. 13 near Siskiyou on October 11, 1923. The train, carrying 115 passengers bound for San Francisco, stopped near the north portal of the tunnel for the usual brake tests preparatory to the descent down the summit.

As the train started, two men appeared from behind a boxcar spotted on the nearby siding and boarded the cab of the locomotive. Only moments after the train emerged from the south portal, it suddenly stopped. The next instant resounded with the explosion that tore away one end of the mail car directly behind the locomotive. When the conductor, who had hurried forward, reached the cab, he found the engineer shot through the forehead, his hand still resting on the throttle. The fireman had also been shot through the head by the desperadoes while he stood, hands upraised, at the cab's side. The conductor only glimpsed the bandits as they disappeared in the distance.

Four long years elapsed and more than a million dollars was spent on the

The Great Train Robbery took place at this exact spot, Tunnel No. 13

miracle of crime detection that finally led to the identification and eventual capture of the criminals, three brothers, twenty-three year old twins Ray and Roy De Autremont and nineteen-year-old Hugh. Their names will long live in American police annals not only for the atrocity of their crime but for the brilliant detection work that made their apprehension possible.

Reward posters like this one were circulated all over the ☞ world in an effort to capture the robbers and murderers.

The Portland Telegram

SERVICE

51st Year 2 Sections—16 Pages PORTLAND, OREGON, THURSDAY EVENING, JUNE 23, 1927 PRICE

DE AUTREMONT BOYS CONFESS;
PRISON MUTINY YET UNBROKEN

328 FELONS IN MINE RUN OUT OF FOOD

Dark Coal Bore in Which Men and 14 Guards Are Locked Remains Silent; Warden Suggests Shots.

EDITORIAL

THE NEW CHARTER

RADIO GIVES TELEGRAM'S PLAN TO ALL

KEX Broadcasts Paper's "Victory Program" for Many Hours; Officials Tell Publication Idea.

Fine Musicians at Telegram Radio Party

TWINS SAY HUGH KILLED ALL VICTIMS

Ray and Roy Break Under Strain; Announce They Are Willing to Throw the Blame on Brother.

The Merlin station, built in Grants Pass, was moved on a flatcar in 1896 or 1897 to its present location by the SP. (George B. Abdill Collection).

Mud was not uncommon in front of the early Oregon railroad stations, as illustrated by this 1902 scene of Merlin.

Oregon & California Railroad motive power shown in front of the station, 1890, Grants Pass, Oregon

Grants Pass station force in 1890: G. P. Jester, agent (in the white suit); Clarence Purdon, chief clerk (nearest the ticket window); R. K. Montgomery, day operator (in the black sleeves); and William Taylor, warehouseman (directly behind Jester).

This photograph, taken in 1900, shows the arrival of the daily passenger train at Medford. The growing and prosperous city is located in the heart of the Rogue River Valley, an area, Joaquin Miller aptly referred to as "America's Italy." The Oregon & California Railroad reached Medford in 1884 and, with the opening of the line between Portland and California, the city has seen a heavy growth each year.

ASHLAND (O&C–SP)

Ashland is the division point and the half-way mark between Portland and San Francisco, the last large city in Oregon before crossing the state line into California. It was here in 1887 where the golden spike was driven connecting the Oregon & California Railroad with the line building up from the south. At last, the two great western coastal states were connected by twin bands of steel.

The chief dispatcher's office in Ashland, 1895. The operation of all trains in southern Oregon was controlled from this office. G. C. Morris (far left) was the chief dispatcher, and Cliff Thomas (far right) was the trick dispatcher.

In 1900, the California Express Train No. 15 stopped for about thirty minutes to service the cars, refill the drinking water, and allow the passengers to stretch their legs on the station platform. This train left Portland at 8:00 P.M. and arrived in Ashland at noon the following day. The deluxe train carried Pullman sleepers, chair cars, and a diner.

Only a few of the trains making the run up and down the coast had dining cars. The station at Ashland included a restaurant that served the traveling public. The long, clean tables were always ready for immediate use. The wicker chairs had hatshelves underneath, and extending downward from the ceiling were festoons of flypaper. In 1900, a complete home-cooked meal could be secured for 50¢, and the menu was always the same—chicken fricassee.

CHAPTER 4

OREGON & CALIFORNIA RAILROAD—WESTSIDE DIVISION (SP)

Ben Holladay's Oregon Central Railroad reached St. Joseph, near McMinnville and forty-two miles from Portland, on November 3, 1872. Although it had been intended to build this line on to a connection with the O&C at Junction City, the terminus remained at St. Joseph until 1879. In that year Henry Villard completed the railroad to Corvallis by way of McMinnville and Independence under the newly renamed Western Oregon Railroad Company. In 1881, the name was again changed to Oregon & California Railroad—Westside Division.

Note the three different names of the line in 1879-80-81, but the same superintendent for all.

St. Joseph station in 1913

INDEPENDENCE

Hundreds of carloads of hops moved annually through this station some years back, but traffic has decreased significantly as fewer and fewer hops are grown in the state.

On hand for the arrival of Train No. 102 in 1914 are farmers with their wagons, many of the local citizens, and a horse-drawn cab representing Independence's one hotel. The arrival of the train was an important event.

Train No. 102 left Corvallis 1:15 P.M.
    Stopped Independence   2:14 P.M.
Arrived Whiteson   3:10 P.M.

At this point the passengers would transfer to Red Electric Train No. 102, which left Whiteson at 3:30 P.M. and arrived Portland at 6:05 P.M. Three years later, the electrification program was extended from Whiteson to Corvallis, passing through Independence.

The Independence agency was staffed for many years by R. K. Montgomery, Paul Sterling, Shirley Roland, and Walter Hilton.

Train No. 102 arrives at Independence in 1914

Bottom left, Shirley E. Roland, the agent at Independence; *bottom right,* a new Western Oregon Railroad schedule, effective the summer of 1880.

WESTERN OREGON RAILROAD.

TIME SCHEDULE No. 3,

To Take Effect on Sunday June 20, 1880, at 12 o'clock noon.

For the government and information of employees only: the Company reserve the right to vary therefrom as circumstances may require.

☞ OBSERVE RULES CAREFULLY.   IMPORTANT CHANGES HAVE BEEN MADE. ☜

BOUND SOUTH.						STATIONS.			BOUND NORTH.			
No. 7.	No. 5.	No. 3. FREIGHT.	No 1. MAIL.						No. 2. MAIL.	No. 4. FREIGHT.	No. 6.	No. 8.
		6.30 A.M. LV.	8.00 A.M. LV.			PORTLAND s	2	97	3.30 P.M. AR.	5.00 P.M. AR.		
			8.17	5	2	FOURTH ST. BRIDGE.	4	95	3.00			
		7.10	8.35	6	4	SUMMIT.	6	91	2.45	2.20		
		7.50	9.00	12	6	BEAVERTON	4	85	2.20	1.40		
		8.18	9.20	16	4	REEDVILLE.	3	81	2.05	1.17		
		8.35	9.30	19	3	NEWTON	2	78	1.55	1.05		
		8.50	9.40	21	2	HILLSBORO s	3	76	1.47	12.57		
		9.15	9.55	24	3	CORNELIUS s	2	73	1.35	12.40		
		9.25	10.03	26	2	FOREST GROVE	2	71	1.27	12.30		
		9.35	10.10	28	2	DILLEY'S	4	69	1.20	12.20		
		10.05	10.25	32	4	GASTON.	2	65	1.05	12.05 P.M.		
		10.20	10.35	34	2	WAPATO.	6	63	12.52	11.52		
		10.55	10.52	40	6	NORTH YAMHILL	3	57	12.35	11.28		
		11.10	11.02	43	3	CARLTON	3	54	12.22	11.10 AR. 11.02 LV.		
		11.35	11.18	47	4	ST. JOSEPH.	3	50	12.05 P.M.	10.35		
11.50		11.30 AR. 11.50 LV.	40	3		McMINNVILLE s	3	47	11.50 LV. 11.30 AR.	10.20		
13.10 P.M.		13.05	51	4		CROSSING W.V.R.R	3	43	11.15	10.00		
13.35		13.15	57	6		AMITY.	5	40	11.05	9.45		
		12.55	12.37	62	5	McCOY'S	8	35	10.45	9.20		
		1.15	1.12	70	8	DERRY	6	27	10.15	8.40		
		2.05	1.35	76	6	INDEPENDENCE s	1	21	9.55	8.10		
		2.30	2.00	81	5	PARKER'S	3	16	9.35	7.43		
		2.40	2.05	84	3	SOAP CREEK	1	13	9.25	7.33		
		2.55	2.15	87	3	WELL'S	1	10	9.10	7.15		
						MT. VIEW						
		3.10 P.M. AR.	3.00 P.M. AR.	97	11	CORVALLIS s			8.30 A.M. LV.	6.30 A.M. LV.		

J. BRANDT, Superintendent, Portland.

Purchased by the railroad around the turn of the century for use as a station, this two-story building had previously been a hotel—one with a doubtful reputation.

Bottom left, for many years this small but modern structure served as the ticket office, while the older, larger building was relegated to use as a freight house. Bottom right, V. L. Irvine, McMinnville's agent.

CHAPTER 5

HENRY VILLARD AND THE OR&N

Henry Villard entered the railroad field representing the German bondholders who foreclosed on Ben Holladay when he failed to meet his indebtedness for the Oregon & California Railroad. Villard took over the line in 1873 and soon saw the tremendous potential of a total transportation system for Oregon.

He systematically purchased all the important means of transportation, both water and rail, giving him nearly complete control of the systems in the state. The ease and rapidity with which Villard and his friends raised money to buy these operations was without precedent, and he climbed quickly to the first rank of world financiers. In 1879 he organized the Oregon Railway & Navigation Company, comprised of the companies he had secured:

• The Oregon Steamship Company—a fleet of ocean steamers.

• The Oregon Steam Navigation Company—river steamboats, docks, barges.

• Willamette Transportation Locks Company—canals and locks at Oregon City around the falls of the Willamette River; also some steamships.

• Walla Walla & Columbia River Railroad—thirty-two miles of narrow gauge track built from Wallula on the Columbia River to Walla Walla.

• Dalles & Deschutes Railroad—portage around the Dalles.

• Cascade Portage Railroad—portage railroad around the lower Cascades of the Columbia River.

Henry Villard

And, of course, Villard controlled the O&C, a line running from Portland to Roseburg and to St. Joseph near McMinnville, forfeited by Ben Holladay.

What Villard had most to fear was the invasion by other lines into the territory then occupied exclusively by his companies. Most threatening were the Cen-

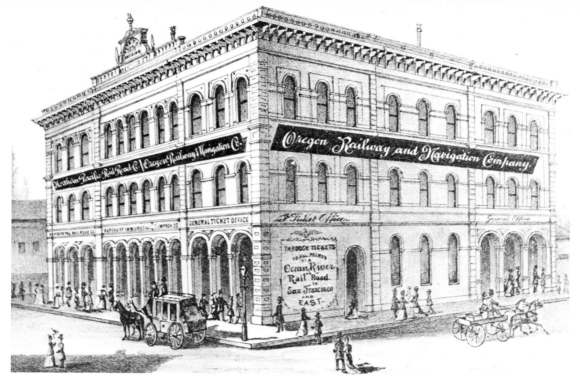

Located on the west side in Portland, this three-story structure was built in 1883 and housed the headquarters of "Villard's Lines." Passengers traveling east or south purchased their rail tickets here. They used the ferry to cross the Willamette River, boarding rail cars on the east side. After April 13, 1887, the railroad bridge was open across the Willamette, allowing trains access to the west side.

tral Pacific from the south, the Union Pacific from the east, and the Northern Pacific from the north.

During the next few years, Villard moved fast. A standard gauge line was constructed from Wallula to Celilo, a distance of 100 miles. Leases were obtained for control of the Oregonian Railway Company, Ltd., the narrow-gauge line in the Willamette Valley, thus preventing it from being secured by competition. Trackage was built along the Oregon side of the Columbia River.

Northern Pacific resumed construction from Lake Pend D'Oreille, Idaho, to the confluence of the Columbia and Snake Rivers, and it was reasonable to believe they would continue on down the north bank of the Columbia River to

Portland paralleling the OR&N on the opposite side. So Villard made an agreement with the NP to operate their trains into Portland over the OR&N tracks from Wallula.

In 1883, transcontinental line was opened using the Portland-to-Wallula tracks, connecting with the NP's. In 1884, a second transcontinental line was opened, using the OR&N to Huntington connecting with the Oregon Short Line and The Union Pacific.

By the latter part of 1883, the securities of the "Villard Lines" were valued in excess of $200,000,000. From the time of his election to the presidency of the O&C to the completion of the NP in September, 1883, his career had been wonderfully successful. He had made

During the 1880s the river division was an important part of the OR&N.

the railroad system in the state of Oregon almost entirely his own.

He had borrowed, however, once too often, and the day of reckoning was due. At last, when he attempted to raise a few millions to meet some deficits, he suffered a defeat with which even he could not cope. On the verge of bankruptcy, there was nothing left for him but to retire from his official connection with the properties he had created.

After Villard's resignation, the UP was able to secure a long term lease on the OR&N, assuring a nearly permanent subsidiary status for the OR&N from then onward.

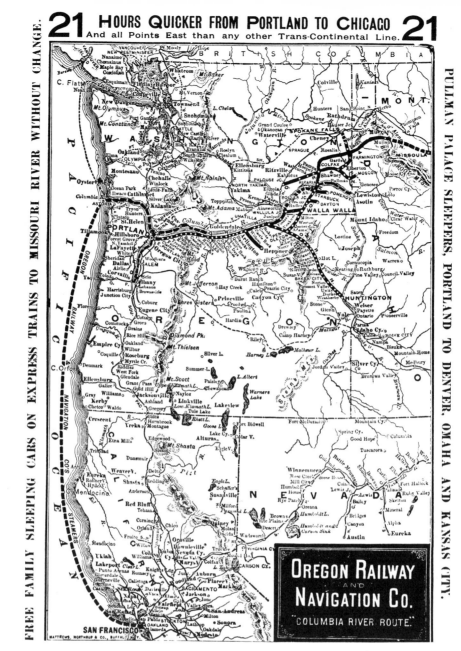

FREE FAMILY SLEEPING CARS ON EXPRESS TRAINS TO MISSOURI RIVER WITHOUT CHANGE.

PULLMAN PALACE SLEEPERS, PORTLAND TO DENVER, OMAHA AND KANSAS CITY.

OREGON RAILWAY AND NAVIGATION CO.
"COLUMBIA RIVER ROUTE."

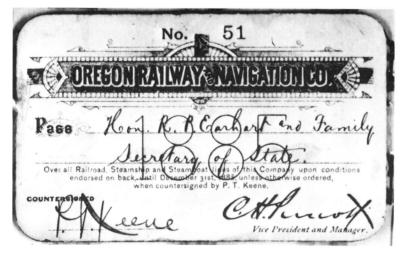

Secretary of State Earhart's family pass on the multiple transportation systems of the OR&N, was issued when the company was at the height of its power, in 1885.

PORTLAND TO THE EAST
VIA THE
OREGON RAILWAY & NAVIGATION
AND
NORTHERN PACIFIC LINE.

CONDENSED THROUGH TIME TABLE.

STATIONS	Daily	Sun	Mon	Tues	Wed	Thur	Fri	Sat
Leave Portland	3 00 P.M.	Sun	Mon	Tues	Wed	Thur	Fri	Sat
" East Portland	3 30 "	"	"	"	"	"	"	"
" Bonneville	6 00 "	"	"	"	"	"	"	"
" Dalles	9 10 "	"	"	"	"	"	"	"
" Umatilla Junc.	1 35 A.M.	Mon	Tues	Wed	Thur	Fri	Sat	Sun
Arrive Wallula Junction	2 40 "	"	"	"	"	"	"	"
Leave Wallula Junction	3 10 A.M.	"	"	"	"	"	"	"
Arrive Ainsworth	3 47 "	"	"	"	"	"	"	"
" Pasco Junct	3 55 "	"	"	"	"	"	"	"
" Palouse Junction	5 25 "	"	"	"	"	"	"	"
Leave Palouse Junction	7 00 A.M.	Mon	Tues	Wed	Thur	Fri	Sat	Sun
Arrive Colfax	2 30 P.M.	"	"	"	"	"	"	"
" Moscow	5 45 "	"	"	"	"	"	"	"
Leave Palouse Junction	5 25 A.M.	"	"	"	"	"	"	"
Arrive Ritzville	7 28 "	"	"	"	"	"	"	"
" Sprague	8 40 "	"	"	"	"	"	"	"
" Cheney	9 54 "	"	"	"	"	"	"	"
" Spokane Falls	10 45 "	"	"	"	"	"	"	"
" Rathdrum	11 55 "	"	"	"	"	"	"	"
" Heron	3 50 P.M.	"	"	"	"	"	"	"
" Missoula	1 00 A.M.	Tues	Wed	Thur	Fri	Sat	Sun	Mon
" Garrison	4 50 "	"	"	"	"	"	"	"
Leave Garrison	6 15 A.M.	"	"	"	"	"	"	"
Arrive Butte	8 40 "	"	"	"	"	"	"	"
" Helena	7 50 "	"	"	"	"	"	"	"
" Bozeman	12 40 P.M.	"	"	"	"	"	"	"
" Livingston	2 24 "	"	"	"	"	"	"	"
Leave Livingston	2 35 P.M.	"	"	"	"	"	"	"
Arrive Cinnabar	5 20 "	"	"	"	"	"	"	"

Direct connection is here made with stage lines into the Yellowstone National Park. See inside pages

STATIONS	Daily							
Leave Livingston	2 20 P.M.	Tues	Wed	Thur	Fri	Sat	Sun	Mon
" Billings	7 15 "	"	"	"	"	"	"	"
" Miles City	1 58 A.M.	Wed	Thur	Fri	Sat	Sun	Mon	Tues
" Glendive	5 40 "	"	"	"	"	"	"	"
" Medora	8 36 "	"	"	"	"	"	"	"
" Mandan	3 15 P.M.	"	"	"	"	"	"	"
" Bismarck	5 00 "	"	"	"	"	"	"	"
" Jamestown	9 15 "	"	"	"	"	"	"	"
" Sanborn	10 11 "	"	"	"	"	"	"	"
" Casselton	12 09 A.M.	Thur	Fri	Sat	Sun	Mon	Tues	Wed
" Fargo	1 20 "	"	"	"	"	"	"	"
" Moorhead	1 23 "	"	"	"	"	"	"	"
" Glyndon	1 46 "	"	"	"	"	"	"	"
" Brainerd	7 10 "	"	"	"	"	"	"	"
" Sauk Rapid	9 15 "	"	"	"	"	"	"	"
" Minneapolis	11 50 "	"	"	"	"	"	"	"
Arrive St. Paul	12 25 P.M.	"	"	"	"	"	"	"
Leave St. Paul	1 40 P.M.	"	"	"	"	"	"	"
Arrive Milwaukee	3 40 A.M.	Fri	Sat	Sun	Mon	Tues	Wed	Thur
"	7 00 "	"	"	"	"	"	"	"

Pullman Sleeping Cars Portland to St. Paul and Minneapolis without change.

Emigrant Sleeping Cars Wallula Junction to St. Paul without change.

Pullman Sleeping Cars connect in Union Depot at St. Paul and Minneapolis for Chicago without change.

Dining Cars from Wallula Junction to St. Paul for all meals. Meals, 75c. each.

THIRTY MINUTES for Supper at Bonneville. Meals, 75c. each.

THROUGH TICKETS will be accepted on the O. R. & N. Steamers between Portland and Dalles, if passengers prefer to go that way.

Close connections made in Chicago for New York, Boston, Montreal and all eastern cities.

PORTLAND TO THE EAST
VIA THE
OREGON RAILWAY & NAVIGATION
AND
UNION PACIFIC (OREGON SHORT LINE.)

CONDENSED THROUGH TIME TABLE.

STATIONS	Daily	Sun	Mon	Tues	Wed	Thur	Fri	Sat
Leave Portland	3 00 P.M.	Sun	Mon	Tues	Wed	Thur	Fri	Sat
" East Portland	3 30 "	"	"	"	"	"	"	"
" *Bonneville	6 00 "	"	"	"	"	"	"	"
" Dalles	9 10 "	"	"	"	"	"	"	"
" Umatilla Juncta	2 00 A.M.	Mon	Tues	Wed	Thur	Fri	Sat	Sun
" Pendleton	4 40 "	"	"	"	"	"	"	"
" *Meacham	8 15 "	"	"	"	"	"	"	"
" La Grande	10 30 "	"	"	"	"	"	"	"
" Baker City	1 05 P.M.	"	"	"	"	"	"	"
Arrive *Huntington	3 30 "	"	"	"	"	"	"	"
Leave Huntington	6 00 P.M.	"	"	"	"	"	"	"
Arrive *Caldwell	9 04 "	"	"	"	"	"	"	"
" Shoshone	3 55 A.M.	Tues	Wed	Thur	Fri	Sat	Sun	Mon
" *Pocatello	7 40 "	"	"	"	"	"	"	"

Passengers for Yellowstone National Park diverge here. See inside pages.

STATIONS	Daily							
Leave Pocatello	8 25 A.M.	Tues	Wed	Thur	Fri	Sat	Sun	Mon
Arrive Ogden	4 50 P.M.	"	"	"	"	"	"	"
" Salt Lake City	7 30 "	"	"	"	"	"	"	"
Leave Pocatello	8 10 A.M.	Tues	Wed	Thur	Fri	Sat	Sun	Mon
Arrive *Cokeville	1 30 P.M.	"	"	"	"	"	"	"
" Granger	4 40 "	"	"	"	"	"	"	"
" *Green River	6 35 "	"	"	"	"	"	"	"
" Rawlins	12 40 A.M.	Wed	Thur	Fri	Sat	Sun	Mon	Tues
" *Laramie	7 20 "	"	"	"	"	"	"	"
Arrive Cheyenne	10 10 "	"	"	"	"	"	"	"
Arrive Denver	2 55 P.M.	Wed	Thur	Fri	Sat	Sun	Mon	Tues
Leave Cheyenne	10 30 A.M.	"	"	"	"	"	"	"
Arrive *Sidney	3 25 P.M.	"	"	"	"	"	"	"
" Denver Junct'n	1 50 "	"	"	"	"	"	"	"
" *North Platte	8 00 "	"	"	"	"	"	"	"
" Kearney Junct'n	11 45 "	"	"	"	"	"	"	"
" Grand Island	1 40 A.M.	Thur	Fri	Sat	Sun	Mon	Tues	Wed
" Central City	2 34 "	"	"	"	"	"	"	"
" Columbus	4 07 "	"	"	"	"	"	"	"
" Fremont	5 55 "	"	"	"	"	"	"	"
" Omaha	7 50 "	"	"	"	"	"	"	"
Arrive Council Bluffs	8 15 "	"	"	"	"	"	"	"
Leave Council Bluffs	9 50 A.M.	Fri	Sat	Sun	Mon	Tues	Wed	Thur
Arrive Chicago	7 00 "	"	"	"	"	"	"	"
Leave Denver	8 05 P.M.	Wed	Thur	Fri	Sat	Sun	Mon	Tues
Arrive Wakeney	7 02 A.M.	Thur	Fri	Sat	Sun	Mon	Tues	Wed
" *Ellis	7 50 "	"	"	"	"	"	"	"
" Hays City	8 13 "	"	"	"	"	"	"	"
" Russell	9 01 "	"	"	"	"	"	"	"
" Ellsworth	10 13 "	"	"	"	"	"	"	"
" Salina	11 11 "	"	"	"	"	"	"	"
" *Abilene	12 08 P.M.	"	"	"	"	"	"	"
" Topeka	3 35 "	"	"	"	"	"	"	"
Arrive Kansas City	5 45 "	"	"	"	"	"	"	"
Leave Kansas City	6 45 P.M.	Fri	Sat	Sun	Mon	Tues	Wed	Thur
Arrive Chicago	2 30 P.M.	"	"	"	"	"	"	"

Pullman Sleeping Cars from Portland to Council Bluffs without change.

Emigrant Sleeping Cars Huntington to Council Bluffs without change.

Pullman Sleeping Cars connect in Union Depots at Council Bluffs and Kansas City for Chicago without change.

Thirty minutes for supper at Bonneville.

*Trains stop for meals at all stations marked thus. Meals at all hotel stations, 75c. each.

Through Tickets will be accepted on the O. R. & N. Steamers between Portland and Dalles if passengers prefer to go that way.

Close connections are made in Chicago for New York, Boston, Montreal and all eastern cities.

This is one of the first public timetables of the Oregon Railroad & Navigation Company, issued in September 1886. Both through schedules from Portland to Chicago are listed: OR&N to Wallula, and NP east; and OR&N to Huntington, OSL-UP east. During this period, Henry Villard was maintaining strong and friendly ties with the Northern Pacific Railway. But the following year, after Villard resigned, the new president abandoned the old policy and entered into an alliance with the Union Pacific, leasing them the holdings of the OR&N.

"Leaving the Union Station in Portland on an OR&N train we cross the Willamette River on the Steel Bridge and ascend an old water course in the east side of the city (Sullivans Gulch)."

"At the summit we see Rocky Butte on our left, and the train quickens its speed as we roll along the track through fertile alluvial plains, through FAIRVIEW, . . ." (Ben Maxwell photo)

". . . and on to the Columbia River at TROUTDALE. Just beyond Troutdale we cross the Sandy River, which issues from a vast glacier on the south side of Mount Hood. This stream is the scene of the annual run of smelt, when millions of these tiny succulent fish are netted by the thousands of people who line both banks. We are at the entrance of the Columbia River gorge. . . . Soon we will see Multnomah Falls and all of its beauty. . . ." (Union Pacific photo) (from OR&N advertising material).

The Multnomah Falls station in 1900 was an open air building offering protection from the Oregon rains. Since there was no road to the falls and no automobiles, many people used the train from Portland, spending the day picnicking and enjoying the awesome beauty of the location. *Opposite,* the small, protective station of earlier days was replaced in 1925 by a large chalet. And automobiles could reach this spectacular scene via the highway.

This is Bonneville's interesting Victorian-style station in 1882. The town was named after one of America's great characters, Captain L. E. Benjamin Bonneville, who was made famous by Washington Irving's immortal classic, *The Adventures of Captain Bonneville*. Nearby, the U.S. Government built the Bonneville Dam in 1935. (Union Pacific photo).

OR&N Train No. 81 Limited Mail, eastbound, stopping at Hood River. (Train No. 81 left Portland at 10:00 A.M. and arrived in Hood River at 11:55 A.M.) The station at left is that of the Mount Hood Railroad. Directly behind it can be seen the tower of the Mount Hood Hotel. The OR&N station is nearly concealed by the locomotive.

This station, in a classic Bavarian design used for the larger agencies, is the OR&N station at Hood River. The agent and his family had their living quarters above the main floor.

This restaurant facility, shown here in 1900, was built by the OR&N and operated by "Grandma" Munra from 1894 to 1902. Inside was a huge fireplace and dining room. In front is "Grandma" Katherine Sterrett Munra.

This crowd gathered for the farm demonstration train in 1912 at Mosier, . . .

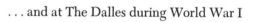

. . . at Echo, . . .

. . . at Hermiston prior to World War I, . . .

. . . and at The Dalles during World War I

Hot Lake, Indian legend tells us, was set aside as a peace ground by medicine men of the surrounding tribes. As a place of peace, rest, and cure for their sick, the curative powers of Hot Lake belonged, so they said, to all Indians. No Indian war has ever taken place here. Today it is the sight of a sanatorium and rest home for the "golden-agers." This photo was taken in 1912.

In 1912 as now, Stanfield is a small farm community along the railroad

This is the old station in Pendleton of 1900

The "Round-up City of the West" built a new railroad station in 1950

The Umatilla station as it looked about 1910. It is here that the Umatilla River empties into the mighty Columbia. Prior to 1882 when the OR&N built into this region, Umatilla Landing—as it was then called—was the gateway to the whole of eastern Oregon. All freight shipments had to be transported by boat to Umatilla, and thence by stage to inland points. (G. B. Abdill Collection)

This unique log cabin station was located in eastern Umatilla County and served as the stopping point for the popular resort at the hot springs. Originally called Gibbon, this scene shows the station in 1903, after it had been renamed Bingham Springs. Apparently dissatisfied with the new name, the residents at last returned the old name to their community, and as Gibbon it is known now.

Milton, about 1914

Bridal Veil, 1914

This photo, taken in 1884, shows one of the first trains into the Grande Ronde Valley and the small settlement of La Grande. (Union Pacific photo)

LA GRANDE (OR&N–UP)

By around 1883, the Grande Ronde Valley folk had become impatient for a railroad. Able to wait no longer, they organized the Columbia River and Blue Mountain Railroad Company to construct a line from La Grande to Umatilla Landing, on the Columbia River. Some grading had been done on the Umatilla end, probably with the idea of ensnaring the big companies' interest. At last, Henry Villard assured the people of La Grande that a railroad would be forthcoming soon.

The city gave the OR&N the property from Oro Dell (a small part of La Grande today) to Hot Lake. When the railroad construction crews reached Oro Dell in late August 1882, one of the survey crew approached the chief engineer and asked him if he could use his influence to find a farm and a mid-wife nearby. The crew member's wife, who assisted with the cooking in the railroad "traveling diner" that fed the crews, had gone into labor. The crew halted work for some thirty minutes until such a need could be filled, and Edward A. Culp was born on August 26 in a small farm home near Oro Dell.

La Grande's present station, the Union Pacific Depot

The North Coast gasoline motors stopping at La Grande on their way to Spokane

Baker City in the late 1880s

Huntington is a railroad man's town—a division point—the end of the Oregon Railroad & Navigation Company's lines and the beginning of the Oregon Short Line. In the center of this 1884 photo can be seen the large, two-story railroad station that served as a ticket office, telegraph office, hotel, dining room, and the general quarters for railroad crews laying over for a return trip. Today this building houses the Pacific Hotel, Mrs. Gramse, Proprietor. (Union Pacific photo)

CHAPTER 6

THE JOSEPH BRANCH (OR&N–UP)
La Grande to Joseph

This eighty-three mile branch line was built from La Grande to Elgin through Indian Valley in 1889. It was extended into Joseph in the fall of 1908. In addition to handling numerous logging trains, it was the route by which to reach Wallowa Lake State Park and the beautiful Wallowa Mountains. It was in those mountains and valleys that Chief Joseph, leader of the Nez Perce Indians recognized as one of the greatest thinkers, statesmen, and generals in American history, made his stand. His efforts to keep the Wallowa country as a home for his people, though tragic and futile, were heroic.

UNION RAILROAD at Cove, Oregon, in 1908 then operating as CENTRAL RAILWAY OF OREGON. Today this small two and a half mile line operates from Union Junction on the Union Pacific Railroad to the town of Union. The line handles forest products almost exclusively. The town of Union back in the 80s was a rival to La Grande for the county seat of Union County. The OR&N in building their railroad through the Grande Ronde Valley passed through the city of La-Grande but missed the town of Union. This action resulted in La Grande securing the county seat and becoming the larger and more important city. The town of Union would not be left out so they constructed their own ten miles of trackage from the OR&N main line at Union Junction to Cove passing through Union. The Cove to Union portion was abandoned in 1927. The line went through many ownerships and changes of names, some of these were: Union Street & Suburban Railway, Union Cove & Valley Railway, and Central Railway of Oregon.

The Enterprise station about 1910

A crew poses for the camera in historic Wallowa, about 1910.

A crowd gathered for the farm demonstration train at Heppner in 1907

THE HEPPNER BRANCH
(OR&N–UP)

This forty-five mile branch line, built in 1889, leaves the OR&N mainline at Heppner Junction and ends at the town of Heppner. June 14, 1903 is a date the people of Heppner and Morrow County will never forget. A cloudburst flooded an upper canyon and came down Willow Creek into Heppner, taking the lives of some 200 people. Destroying two miles of railroad, it continued down Willow Creek through Ione, but the people there were warned in time to avoid any loss of life.

The station at Ione in 1960

CHAPTER 7

THE NORTHERN PACIFIC RAILWAY (BN)

The Northern Pacific owns, in addition to its other trackage, forty-five miles in Umatilla County extending from the Washington state line through Athena into Pendleton. This line was originally built as the Oregon & Washington Territory Railroad, better known as the Hunt Railroad, named after its builder and promoter, George W. Hunt.

In 1892, the line fell into receivership and the Northern Pacific secured control, operating the line for a while as the Washington & Columbia River Railroad, serving some of the richest wheat fields in the state.

Northern Pacific advertising poster of 1890

For nearly thirty years Goble was an important station on the Northern Pacific Railway. It was from here, on the Oregon side of the Columbia River, that trains were ferried across to Kalama, Washington, for the continuation of the rail trip to Tacoma and Seattle. When the Interstate Bridge was built around 1911, Goble's importance began to wane. These photographs, taken in 1900, show the arrival of a train at Goble and the careful trip down the incline to the waiting ferry, *Tacoma*, that will take engine and all across the Columbia.

CHAPTER 8

NARROW GAUGE RAIL LINES IN THE WILLAMETTE VALLEY (SP)

The narrow gauge lines in the Willamette Valley were built to serve areas missed by the Oregon & California Railroad Company, and they were constructed without the aid of the Federal Land Grant.

DAYTON, SHERIDAN & GRAND RONDE RAILROAD COMPANY

A small group of farmers coming from Sheridan, Willamina, Bellevue, Perrydale, and Dallas met in 1877 to discuss possibilities of building a railroad into their respective areas. Without rail service, these farmers found it impossible to compete with those located along the railroads and waterways.

The meeting resulted in the incorporation of the Dayton, Sheridan & Grand Ronde Railroad Company. Rolling stock and metal fastings were purchased, and some twenty miles of trackage was constructed from Sheridan to Dayton on the Yamhill River. Although these farmers pledged their personal wealth, most of it was in land. Actual cash was scarce, and soon the line, for lack of money, was taken over by its creditors.

THE OREGONIAN RAILWAY COMPANY, LIMITED

A group of Scot capitalists, headed by the Earl of Airlie, paid off the indebtedness of the DS&GR in 1879 and took over its operation. The line was renamed the Oregonian Railway Company, Limited, and the terminal at Dayton on the Yamhill River was moved to Fulquartz Landing on the larger and more navigable Willamette River. On the opposite side of the Willamette from Fulquartz Landing they established Ray's Landing, another rail terminal. From this point trackage was constructed through St. Paul, Woodburn, Silverton, and on to Brownsville and Coburg. Headquarters for the Oregonian Railway were at Dundee, a spot selected on higher ground above Fulquartz Landing and named after the city in Scotland.

Steamboat service left Portland in the morning and reached Fulquartz and Ray's Landings in the early afternoon, making connections with the trains for destinations into the Willamette Valley.

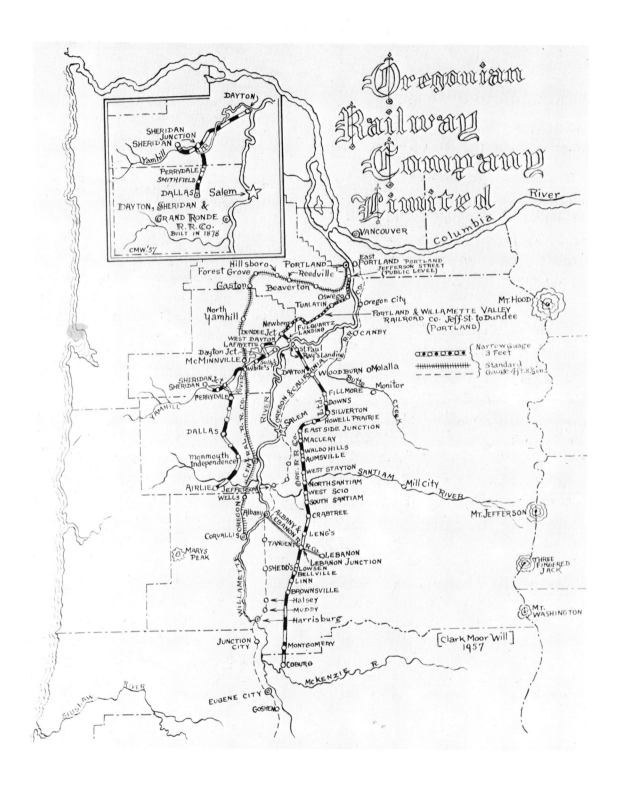

RULES AND REGULATIONS

—OF THE—

OREGONIAN RAILWAY COMPANY, Limited.

1—The clock in the Superintendent's office at Dayton and Portland will be the standard time, and conductors and engineers will regulate their time pieces by it daily.

2—Passenger trains have the indefinite right of the road against freight trains.

3—Freight trains must be kept entirely out of the way of passenger trains, and must be clear of the main track at every station where they are to meet, or be passed by a passenger train, at least five minutes before the schedule time of such train. Freight trains must in no case run beyond a station in the direction of an approaching train, or occupy the main track at a station, without keeping a flagman ahead at least one thousand yards to warn the approaching train.

4—At meeting points, or where trains are expected to be met, conductors will allow five minutes for delayed trains, on account of the possible variation of watches. This allowance must be made at each succeeding station, until the expected train or trains have been passed. Northward bound trains will wait thirty minutes *after their own leaving time* at a meeting station, or where they may be expected, for southward bound trains of the same class; and up to this time the southward bound train will be entitled to the road. After the expiration of the 30 minutes the southward bound train will lose its right, and the northward bound train, after waiting five minutes longer, will proceed, keeping 35 minutes behind *its* own time, until the expected train or trains are passed.

5—No portion of the 5 minutes allowed for variation of watches must be used by trains running in either direction.

6—No passenger train will be allowed to run without a bell cord running from the rear coach to the signal bell in the cab of the engine, to which the cord must be attached.

7—Conductors of Construction or Work trains will report each night their limits for the following day, and obtain their running orders. Should it be necessary to run beyond those limits, they will ask for further orders; in case the line should not be in working order, they will proceed only by Flagging in all obscure places.

8—At all places of meeting, the Ruling train will be entitled to the main track.

9—Conductors will be held personally responsible for the proper adjustment of all switches used by their train.

10—No train will be allowed to leave a station ahead of its schedule time, except by special orders from the Superintendent or Train Dispatcher.

11—*Gravel and all special and irregular trains* must give all regular trains, and trains running under a Red Flag, a clear track; they must be on siding out of the way, ten minutes before regular trains are due at the station.

12—Track men must use the utmost caution at all times, as under the telegraph system of working the road a train may be expected at any moment. At all times when a rail has to be taken out, or other work done, a man must be sent out in each direction, with proper signals, to stop approaching trains, if work is to be done which will render the track unsafe for trains to pass at their usual speed. A stationary Red Flag must be set at least six hundred yards from the spot.

13—No train shall exceed the rates of speed specified in writing on the various bridges and trestles.

14—Section Foremen will appraise all stock that may be killed by trains upon their respective Sections, and forward promptly to the Superintendent's office a full report of the same, giving amount of appraisal, owner's name and place of residence, and also stating whether killed upon owner's land or not.

15—The time indicated in this table is the leaving time for all trains, except when the arriving and leaving time are specified. When there is no meeting point given the leaving time will always be taken for the time trains are to be met, according to Rule No. 4.

16—Engineers must see that their engines are provided with two white and one red lantern, red flags, and all tools necessary in case of accident. No train or engine must be run at night without proper *head light*. They will also be particular and close their ash pan before crossing bridges and trestle work.

17—Conductors are authorized to call on Section Men for assistance in case of accident, and in loading and unloading cars.

18—No train must exceed a speed of four miles per hour while crossing the Willamette river bridge (when completed).

19—Engineers are subject to the orders of the Conductor having charge of the train, but at the same time are held equally responsible with the Conductor in carrying out all the prescribed rules, which are necessary to secure safety.

20—Engineers will sound the whistle at the distance of one-half mile before reaching Stations, and will bring their trains under full control before passing first switch. The bell must be rung eighty rods from Road Crossings, and also while moving about Stations.

21—Engineers will not allow any one not connected with the train to ride on the engine except by permission of the Superintendent or General Manager.

22—*Great care* must be taken to prevent running over *stock*, and trains must come to a *full stop*, "if necessary," to avoid doing so. Engineers will be held to a strict account for any carelessness in killing *stock*.

23—*Conductors* must *report* all delays and *accidents* and the killing of stock of any kind during the trip, giving the locality and all the facts connected with the accident, and kind and description of stock as *fully* as possible.

24—No Conductor in running a train shall assume the rights or take the time of another train, without a special order from the Superintendent or Train Dispatcher.

25—The rear car of every train must be a brake car, and a man must always be stationed on that car. This rule applies to Gravel and Wood trains as well as others.

26—Brakemen must never apply the brakes so tight as to slide the wheels. Conductors will see that this rule is strictly complied with.

27—Conductors will do such switching as may reasonably be required, and in the absence of brakemen look after the brakes.

28—Freight trains will in no case (except by special order) be run over 12 miles per hour.

29—Engineers will sound a long whistle at the distance of three-quarters of a mile before reaching the crossings of the Western Oregon and Oregon & Cal. R. R., and must bring their trains to a full stop before crossing their track.

30—No wood, freight, timber or other material of any kind will be allowed to be piled closer than within five feet of the track.

SIGNALS.

31—A Green Flag by day, or a Green Light by night, displayed at any station, is the signal for telegraph orders, and must not be passed by any train or engine without a train, without coming to a full stop, and the Conductor going to the telegraph office at once to receive such orders as may be there in waiting for him.

32—A stationary Red Flag by day denotes that the track is imperfect, and must be run over with great care. A Red Flag by day or a Red Lantern by night waved upon the track signifies that the train must come to a full stop. The waving of a hat or any like action should be regarded as a signal of danger and NOT PASSED UNNOTICED.

33—A Red Flag by day or a Red Light by night displayed on the front of an engine, indicates that an engine or train is following, which has precisely the same rights as the engine bearing the signal. An extra train or engine following a regular train and properly signaled, must always be considered as a part, and to have all the rights of the leading train, and no more.

34—A White Flag by day, or a White Lantern by night, carried on the front of an engine, indicates that another train or engine is following, which will keep out of the way of all regular trains. Trains under a White Flag, Southward bound, are entitled to the road against Northward bound trains under a similar flag.

35—The Superintendent and Train Dispatcher are the only persons authorized to put out signals for the following trains. Conductors and Engineers carrying such signals, must, without fail, give notice to the Conductor and Engineer of the train they are going to lead that they will do so. They must also call the attention of the Station Agents, Conductors and Engineers having charge of opposing trains and all others interested to the signals, and explain their meaning as far as practicable.

36—A lantern swung across the track is the signal to stop. A lantern swung in a circle is the signal to go ahead. A lantern raised and lowered is to back up.

37—*One blast* of the whistle means to apply the brakes. *Two blasts*, signals to loose the brakes, and *three blasts*, a signal to back. *Four blasts* shall be the signal for switch or calling in flag men. *One stroke* of the cab bell signifies stop; *two* to go ahead, and *three* to back up.

Rules for Running Trains upon Telegraph Orders.

38—All special orders by Telegraph for the movement of trains will be given in writing by the operator, who shall repeat it back with the Conductor's and Engineer's signature, with the prefix "I 13," which means, "I understand," to the office from which the order was received. If correct, the person sending the order will respond, "O. K."—one copy must be given to the Conductor and one to the Engineer, who shall see that they are exact copies of the order signed by them. Both copies shall be signed by the operator.

39—Special orders are to be used by the train only to which they are addressed, and no other train will be allowed to use them. They are to be used against such trains only as are expressly named therein, and an order to run on the time of any particular train must not be taken to run on the time of any other train. All other trains must be run against strictly as per schedule.

40—Any Engineer, leaving a station under special orders, without a copy of the order in his possession, will be held personally responsible for all damage that may result therefrom.

41—When an Agent or Operator receives an order to hold any train for any purpose, he must carry out the order strictly. Conductors and Engineers will respect such orders, and comply with the same in all cases.

42—Operators must remain within hearing of their instruments while trains are due, and at their respective stations. They will also see that their signals are kept in proper order for use at any moment.

43—An order giving a train right to run as an extra or wild train will be of the following form:

No. —— will run to —— as an extra by rule.
(See Rule No. 11.)

44—An order making a definite meeting point is of the following form:

Nos. —— and —— will meet at ——.

45—An order giving one train the right to the road against another to a certain point, until a certain time, is of the following form:

No. —— has to make —— against No. ——.

46—An order giving one train the road against another train, indefinitely, is of the following form:

No. —— will run to —— regardless of No. ——.

47—An order naming any train will include all the sections of such train, unless otherwise specified in the order.

48—No train must run upon telegraph order without the prefix "O. K.," and the name of the person sending it. Should the line fail to work before the Operator has received the "O. K.," he will not deliver such order.

49—Operators will, upon receiving telegraphic orders for expected trains, immediately display the proper signals, as required in Rule 31, and the signal must be taken in as soon as the trains have passed for which they have orders.

By Order of the Board of Directors,

WILLIAM REID,

Local President and General Manager.

PORTLAND, Oregon, 16 June, 1880

The Oregonian Railway Company's Rules and Regulations for the operation of its lines, dated June 16, 1880. Among them: • The maximum speed of freight trains was twelve miles per hour. • At trains' meeting points, five minutes were to be allowed for possible variations in trainmen's watches. • Engineers were warned not to blow the whistle except when necessary, since "too much sounding of the whistle impairs its value as a signal of danger." • Each passenger train was required to have a cord attached to the bell on the locomotive that ran the entire length of the train and attached to the rear car. • The use of "spiritous liquors while on duty" was strictly prohibited. • No engineer was allowed to run at night without a headlight. • The fireman was instructed to close the ash pan when crossing trestles.

☞ READ CAREFULLY.

THESE RULES, REGULATIONS AND TIME TABLES SUPER-
SEDE ALL PREVIOUSLY ISSUED.

OREGONIAN RAILWAY COMPANY

(LIMITED.)

EAST AND WEST SIDE DIVISIONS.

TIME TABLE No. I.

TO TAKE EFFECT MONDAY, JANUARY 10, 1881, AT 6 O'CLOCK A. M.

FOR THE GOVERNMENT AND INFORMATION OF EMPLOYEES ONLY. THE
COMPANY RESERVES THE RIGHT TO VARY THE SAME, AS CIR-
CUMSTANCES MAY REQUIRE.

J. M. FILLMORE,

GENERAL SUPERINTENDENT.

PORTLAND, OREGON.

The Oregonian Railway's first operating timetable.

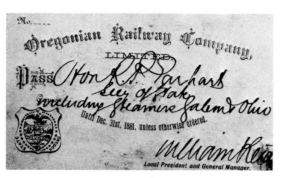

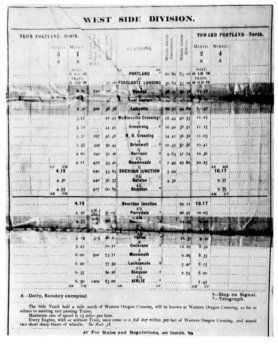

Narrow Gauge, West Side Div., and Portland & Willamette Valley Railway.

49 Pass.	47 Pass.	45 Pass.	43 Pass.	41 Pass.	37 Pass.	35 Pass.	33 Mail	Miles	Trains run Daily, except Sunday.	Miles	34 Mail	36 Pass.	38 Pass.	40 Pass.	44 Pass.	46 Pass.	48 Pass.	50 Pass.
P.M.	P.M.	P.M.	P.M.	P.M.	A.M.	P.M.	A.M.				P.M.	A.M.	A.M.	A.M.	P.M.	P.M.	P.M.	P.M.
*8 35	6 30	5 15	1 55	12 15	7 00	4 30	9 40	0	lv ... **Portland** .. ar	79	3 05	9 30	6 30	8 30	1 30	4 15	6 20	7 40
8 45	6 40	5 25	2 05	12 25	7 10	4 40	9 52	3	...Southern Portland ..	77	2 55	9 20	6 20	8 20	1 20	4 05	6 10	7 30
8 47	6 42	5 27	2 07	12 27	7 12	4 42	9 56	4	.... Fulton	76	2 52	9 18	6 18	8 18	1 18	4 03	6 08	7 28
8 49	6 44	5 29	2 09	12 29	7 14	4 44	10 00	4	.... Cemetery	75	2 49	9 16	6 16	8 16	1 16	4 01	6 06	7 26
8 56	6 51	5 36	2 16	12 36	7 21	4 51	10 08	5	.... Riverside	74	2 40	9 09	6 09	8 09	1 09	3 54	5 59	7 19
9 05	7 00	5 45	2 25	12 45	7 30	5 00	10 20	7	.... Oswego	72	2 30	9 00	6 00	8 00	1 00	3 45	5 50	7 10
P.M.	P.M.	P.M.	P.M.	P.M.	A.M.													
						5 20	10 51	13	........Tualatin.........	66	1 53	8 40						
						5 34	11 24	17	..... Sherwood	62	1 26	8 26						
						5 38	11 38	19	..... Middleton.......	60	1 18	8 22						
						6 05	12 30	26	........Newberg	53	12 30	7 55						
						6 14	1 05	29	.... **Dundee**	51	12 15	7 43						
						6 26	1 35	33	......West Dayton	47	11 25	7 34						
						6 34	1 55	35	..... Lafayette	45	11 10	7 26						
						6 54	2 30	41	.... Brandt's.......	38	10 33	7 06						
						7 02	2 46	43	.... White's	36	10 20	6 58						
						7 27	3 24	50	...... Sheridan Jc.....	29	9 39	6 33						
						7 46		53	.... Ballston.......	32		6 14						
						8 15		57	ar..... **Sheridan** ..lv	33		5 45						
						3 37		53	.... Perrydale	27	9 26							
						4 02		57	.... Smithfield	22	9 02							
						4 38		63	.... Dallas	16	8 27							
						5 20		70	........Monmouth......	9	7 45							
						6 05		79	ar ..... **Airlie** lv	0	7 00							

Additional Trains leave Portland for Oswego at 10.15 A. M., and Saturdays only at 11.30 P. M.

Sunday Trains for Oswego and way stations leave Portland at 9.00 and 11.15 A. M. and 1.00, 2.30, 4.00, 5.30 and 7.30 P. M., arriving at Oswego at 9.30 and 11.45 A. M. and 1.30, 3.00, 4.30, 6.00 and 8.00 P. M.

*Except Saturday and Sunday.

Additional Train leaves Oswego for Portland at 10.55 A. M.

Sunday Trains for Portland and way stations leave Oswego at 8.00 and 10.00 A. M., 12.00 NOON, and 1.40, 2.10, 4.40 and 6.30 P. M., arriving at Portland at 8.30 and 10.30 A. M. and 12.30, 2.10, 3.40, 5.10 and 7.00 P. M.

A timetable issued March, 1893, by the West Side Division and P&WVR

PORTLAND AND WILLAMETTE VALLEY RAILWAY COMPANY

A new company, The Portland & Willamette Valley Railway Company, was formed in 1886 to complete the extension of the narrow gauge from Dundee through Newberg and Oswego and into Portland. This additional trackage eliminated the need for the steamboat service formerly used to bring passengers and freight from Portland to a connection with the Oregonian Railway.

Tensions grew as freight and passenger revenues became inadequate to meet company expenses. The pay car that brought wages to the employees was seen less and less. One conductor—and an honest one—assumed the responsibility of the workers. As he told it, he

would toss the money collected from rail fares into the air inside the coach, and that which balanced on the bell cord was turned over to the railroad, while that which fell to the ground went into his pocket to be paid to the employees along the line.

Revenues continued to drop, and the line fell into receivership. The Scot investors, becoming increasingly con-

It was here in the '80s that the Oregonian Railway Company, Ltd., drove the first spike for their narrow gauge line that would run from Ray's Landing on the Willamette River through St. Paul, Woodburn, Silverton, and on to Coburg. The Silverton Local, SP-129, running over the same track, left Silverton at 2:00 P.M., arrived Salem at 3:00, left at 5:00, arrived Woodburn at 6:20, left at 6:30 to return to Silverton at 7:00 P.M. The photo was taken in 1913.

cerned about their money, granted Henry Villard of the O&C a long-term lease which allowed him complete control of the Oregonian Railway and the P&WV. At Villard's exit from the Oregon railroad scene, the line fell into the hands of the Southern Pacific Company, which converted the trackage into standard gauge and used it for feeder service to their own operations.

Harry Vetter, the last agent in Silverton before the agency was closed.

Located two miles north of Silverton, Downs was a station on the Oregonian Railway's narrow gauge. The tracks had been built very close to the farm of James Down, an early settler in the area. The photo was taken in 1885.

A freight "highballs" through Mt. Angel. This small German-Catholic settlement was originally called Fillmore, after the superintendent of the Oregonian Railway Company, Ltd. St. Mary's Church, still under construction in the background, was finished and dedicated later the same year, 1912.

Upper left, Eugene F. Sperle, the last agent at Mt. Angel. *Upper right,* The Aumsville station, on "The Road of a Thousand Wonders." *Below,* The Aumsville staff in December, 1914: Addie Condit, telegraph operator, and Ross Condit (her brother), the agent.

WEST STAYTON (ORR–SP)

Built in 1883 or 1884 by the Oregonian Railway Company, Ltd., the West Stayton station is still in use today. Although it remains an old wooden structure on the outside, there has been some modernization within. Toilet facilities, for instance, were installed for the first time ten years ago.

This old station's claim to fame is that one of the world's greatest political cartoonists, Homer Calvin Davenport, worked here for the old narrow gauge railroad. During that period he drew a picture of his beloved dog, Duff, on one of the rough wooden walls in the warehouse portion of the station building. Now the drawing has been removed and will be placed in a suitable location for permanent keeping.

In his autobiography, *The Country Boy*, Davenport wrote: "I guess it was when I was about 17 I raised a pup. I liked him more than I did some people and he preferred me to some dogs. I loved him then and I love his memory now. I named him Duff."

The West Stayton station in 1900. Train No. 46 operated from Woodburn to Springfield, leaving Woodburn at 10:59 A.M. and reaching Springfield at 6:45 P.M. A connecting train left Portland at 8:30 A.M. and arrived at Woodburn at 10:27.

Above, Homer Davenport, one of the world's greatest political cartoonists, worked at the West Stayton station as a boy in 1885. *Below*, Henry Beecher Condit, agent for thirty-five years at West Stayton, protected Davenport's drawing of Duff for future historians.

West Stayton's agent, Henry Beecher Condit, awaiting the evening train inside of the station on Christmas evening 1914.

WEST SCIO (ORR–SP)

The Oregonian Railway Company, Ltd., when laying narrow gauge track from Silverton to Coburg, missed the small town of Scio. The line, instead, was built two miles west through a point that became known as West Scio.

Scio's townspeople were disappointed that they were not given a railroad into their community. Finally, with the help of some of SP's track men, they constructed their own railroad from Scio to West Scio. They leased "Old Betsy" from the SP for motive power. She was one of three engines built by the Vulcan

Iron Works of San Francisco in 1862, and had been used to complete the first twenty miles of track from East Portland to Parrott Creek for Ben Holladay's Oregon & California Railroad.

Passengers desiring to make a connection with the train at West Scio would ride over on a flat car pulled by "Old Betsy." It was a nice arrangement, but the state inspectors and the regulatory advisors finally forced Scio to abandon the line in 1904. "Old Betsy" was returned to her owners for scrapping.

Above, The station of West Scio in 1890. *Below,* "Old Betsy," leased by the determined citizenry of Scio for their motive power on the two miles of track to West Scio. Andrew Hagey posed in the cab with Fred Daly in the gangway, sometime in the 1890s.

Train No. 98 rolls into Brownsville, one of the oldest towns in the Willamette Valley

BROWNSVILLE (ORR–SP)

Brownsville, one of the oldest cities in the Willamette Valley, was a farming community. Countless colonists from the East went there to make their homes. For a time the town was served by the narrow gauge line of the Oregonian Railway Company, Ltd. In 1890 the mayor of Brownsville and a group of the townspeople joined a work party of SP trackmen—the SP then owned the line—to change the trackage from narrow to standard gauge, thus allowing a free interchange of cars from all railroads.

COLONIST RATES TO BROWNSVILLE, OREGON

Will prevail from all parts of the East and Canada during March and April. Tickets will be on sale daily at the rates named below. See Map showing routes.

From—	Rate.	From—	Rate.	From—	Rate.
Atchison, Kan.	$25.00	Des Moines, Ia.	$27.70	Muskogee, Okla.	$28.35
Atlanta, Ga.	43.55	Detroit, Mich.	38.00	Nashville, Tenn.	37.30
Augusta, Ga.	46.75	Elmira, N. Y.	45.80	New York, N. Y.	50.00
Baltimore, Md.	48.25	Evansville, Ind.	34.00	Oklahoma, Okla.	28.45
Birmingham, Ala.	40.25	Hamilton, Ont.	41.05	Omaha, Neb.	25.00
Bloomington, Ill.	31.20	Hannibal, Mo.	29.00	Peoria, Ill.	30.35
Bristol, Tenn.	44.80	Indianapolis, Ind.	35.15	Philadelphia, Pa.	49.75
Boston, Mass.	49.45	Jacksonville, Fla.	50.75	Pittsburg, Pa.	42.00
Buffalo, N. Y.	42.50	Kansas City, Mo.	25.00	Savannah, Ga.	48.75
Burlington, Ia.	28.50	Knoxville, Tenn.	41.55	Sioux City, Ia.	26.95
Cairo, Ill.	33.75	Leavenworth, Kan.	25.00	Springfield, Ill.	31.00
Charleston, S. C.	48.75	Louisville, Ky.	36.70	St. Joseph, Mo.	25.00
Chicago, Ill.	33.00	Memphis, Tenn.	36.00	St. Louis, Mo.	30.50
Cincinnati, O.	37.40	Milwaukee, Wis.	33.00	St. Paul, Minn.	25.00
Cleveland, O.	39.75	Minneapolis, Minn.	25.00	St. Thomas, Ont.	41.05
Columbia, S. C.	46.75	Mobile, Ala.	42.95	Tallahassee, Fla.	48.55
Columbus, O.	39.15	Montgomery, Ala.	42.95	Toledo, O.	37.30
Council Bluffs, Ia.	25.00	Montreal, Que.	47.70	Toronto, Ont.	41.05
				Washington, D. C.	48.25

FARES CAN BE PREPAID

By a system in general use among railroads the cost of a ticket can be deposited at pleasure with any local ticket agent in Oregon or elsewhere, and the necessary ticket will be furnished to the person named, no matter where the residence may be, in compliance with telegraphic instruction. This enables residents of Brownsville to send for relatives, friends or employes in any part of the East without the inconvenience and delay of correspondence. Local Ticket Agent E. E. Boyd, with whom the deposit should be made, will attend to all details.

Brownsville became such a popular emigrant attraction that the railroads' servicing the town instituted special colonist rates for March and April, 1909.

The Oregonian Railway Company's twenty mile narrow gauge line (acquired from the local farmers of the DS&GR Railway) that ran from Sheridan to Dayton on the Yamhill River and the Oregon & California Railway—Westside Division's standard gauge line (acquired from the Western Oregon Railway Company) that ran from Portland through McMinnville to Corvallis intersected at White's as the town was first known. Of course, the two lines were fierce rivals for the traffic involved, but they made little effort to offer schedules that connected with each other. The hotel at the left was frequently used by rail patrons who were forced to stop overnight in order to make the proper connections between the lines. The photo was taken in 1890.

This etching of Fulton Park station in 1885 shows the quaint community located on the west side of the Willamette, near the western approach of the Sellwood Bridge, about one mile south of the business district of Portland.

The large Jefferson Street Terminal in 1905 can be seen to the right. The extra cars adjacent to the building were reserved for overflow traffic. The Portland and Willamette Valley Railway Company, a narrow gauge line that was a part of the Oregonian Railway Company, Ltd., reached this terminal in 1887. The lines through the Jefferson Street Terminal served many of the wealthy families residing in homes overlooking the Willamette River and brought commuters from Fulton, Riverdale, Rivera, and Oswego into Portland. About 1912, at the time the Red Electric service was introduced, trackage was extended up Jefferson Street to a connection with the Fourth Street Line, giving the terminal users entrance into the heart of Portland and Union Station.

P&WV Railway Terminal and Ticket Office of 1887, located at the foot of Jefferson Street on the westside of Portland, looking south as seen from an early drawing. Today this location would be about the middle of Harbor Drive and just south of the Hawthorne Bridge. Sailing vessels in the background can be seen moored along the docks of the Willamette River.

Portland & Willamette Valley R. R.

Suburban Trains leave Jefferson Street Depot 7.25
9.20, 11.00, 12.30 a. m., 2.00 3.40, 5.20, 6.20, 8.35 p. m.

Return Tickets, 10, 20 and 25 Cents.

Oregonian Railway No. 7 in 1887. The group of four located beside the cab and in front of the
tender are, left to right: Conductor Bob Clark; N. L. "Tack" Butler, Dallas attorney; Si Bennett,
brakeman; Sam Sconlon, engineer, Dallas, Oregon.

The arrival in Dallas in 1910 of the train from Portland

Lower left, Interior of the Dallas station, 1960. At left, Orrin Kelley; at right, Ray Weathers.
Lower right, Floyd Jasper Spooner, Dallas agent for many years.

CHAPTER 9

THE OREGON PACIFIC RAILROAD
The Line That Could Have Changed
Oregon's History

At a time when Benton County extended from Corvallis to the Pacific Ocean, the citizens of the region envisioned a railroad from the Albany-Corvallas area to the tidewater of Yaquina Bay.

Clothing and staples produced in the East were shipped either around the Horn or by rail to San Francisco and thence by water to Oregon. Freighters and clipper ships were towed up the Columbia by steam launch, from Astoria to Portland. Even though it was a hundred miles from the sea, rapidly growing Portland was the shipping center of the state.

Since Yaquina Bay was much closer to California than was Portland via the ocean-river trip, the Benton County people reasoned that freight handled through Yaquina Bay might be carried to Portland more quickly and more cheaply than it was then. And, of course, a railroad from the valley to Yaquina Bay would give the Corvallis folk an advantage over their Portland neighbors.

At about the same time a plan was devised to continue building the Oregon

Pacific Railroad east from Albany, over the Cascades, to a connection with one of the eastern lines, offering the people of Corvallis and Albany their own transcontinental railroad. Colonel Thomas Egerton Hogg came forth as the leading promoter and builder of the OPRR.

The Santiam Canyon and the easy

The Oregon Pacific schedule for 1891

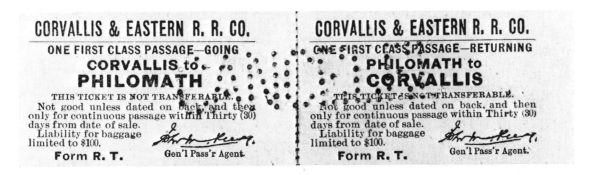

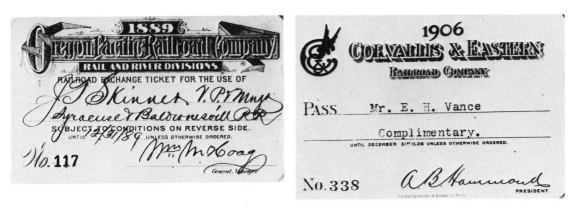

Upper right, Andrew Benoni Hammond purchased the OPR for his lumbering operations, renaming it the Corvallis & Eastern Railroad Company. *Below,* The Oregon Pacific Railroad.

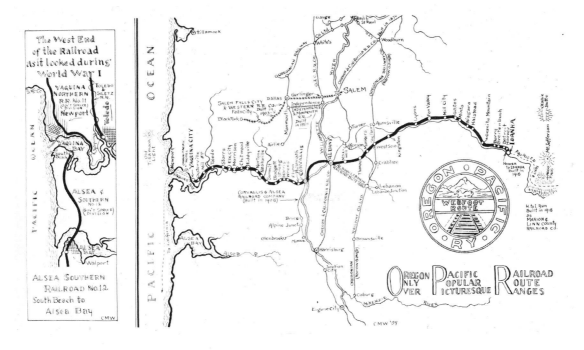

The Corvallis & Eastern Railroad Company did a great deal to promote beach traffic to Newport, on Yaquina Bay. On weekends often six or eight trains were needed to accommodate the large crowds. Since the track ended at Yaquina City, the steamer *Yaquina,* seen in this 1910 photo, carried the crowds the three mile trip across the bay. One of the big events of the day was the evening arrival of a new group of tourists from the valley.

grade through Hogg's Pass in eastern Marion County was decided upon as ideal for railroad building. Although it was a costly plan, monies were secured for the program.

Colonel Hogg constructed 142 miles of railroad, from the Pacific eastward. In the early '90s, the line reached what is today the Detroit Dam area, and halted. It was never to pass this point. Unable

"This is the town of great renown
That lay at the end of the road that Hogg built."

Today one can drive along the bay from Newport to Toledo, pass through Yaquina City, and never know that such a town existed: A town that once boasted a large railroad station (shown in this 1911 photo), a roundhouse, railroad shops, a bank, a three-story hotel, a hardware store, and innumerable homes that dotted the overlooking hill. The railroad had originally intended to build into Newport. But on the news of its coming, Newport's property values began to skyrocket, and her citizens thought that the increased prices could as well be paid by the railroad. In response, Mr. Hogg terminated his line at a place he himself named Yaquina City.

C&E No. 2 Eastbound, arriving Toledo enroute Corvallis and Albany in 1910. William C. Hoeflein, conductor, on steamdome; George Woods, brakeman, on pilot; Engineer Arthur Casteel, standing in engine's gangway. The Toledo station was built in 1892 by the local townspeople from bricks that were brought around the Horn as ship's ballast. After the bricks were unloaded at Yaquina City, the citizenry of Toledo, who were eager to help Colonel Thomas E. Hogg and the OPR, loaded them on a flatcar for their town.

to meet interest payments on its loans, the Oregon Pacific fell into receivership before the end of the century. Andrew Benoni Hammond purchased the line for his lumber interests at a sheriff's sale and renamed it The Corvallis & Eastern Railway Company. Several years later the Southern Pacific took the line over from Hammond.

The lack of adequate planning and

One of the many excursion trains passing through Elk City in 1910

This 1910 photo shows the building that housed both the railroad station, called Morrison, and the Post office, called Pioneer. Some of the stone from the quarry nearby was used to build the Call Building in San Francisco.

know-how defeated the vast undertaking. For one thing, the shallow bar and harbor of Yaquina Bay needed improving. The people of Newport today, nearly a century later, are still waiting for the U.S. Government to complete the needed improvements. And they still dream of being a world shipping center.

The train arrives in Philomath in 1918. The United Brethren Church founded Philomath (pronounced *Phil-a-math*) College here in 1867. The word comes from the Greek, meaning "love of learning." After the coming of the railroad, the name was quite generally pronounced *Flo-math*.

Summit in 1889. The middle building was the Oregon Pacific Railroad station

Summit in 1912

The Corvallis station, shown here in 1914 when it was located at 7th and Washington, was used jointly by the Southern Pacific and the Corvallis & Eastern Railroad. During WWI, this station was moved to 6th Street, between Madison and Monroe. In 1956 the SP sold it to the city of Corvallis, and today it is used as the town jail and police headquarters. Engineer Arthur Casteel is oiling up C&E No. 1 that has just arrived from Yaquina. SP cars can be seen at the rear of the station.

The rear of the Corvallis station. The Wells Fargo office is directly behind the horse-drawn wagon.

ISSUED BY

CORVALLIS & EASTERN R. R. CO.

Good for One Continuous First-Class Passage

TO

Destination written in Coupons attached

Via Route designated in coupons attached, when officially stamped and sold by the Company's Agent.

1st. LIMIT. This ticket will be good only on date of sale stamped on back hereof, or on day following.

2nd. STOP-OVERS. Will not be allowed.

3rd. BAGGAGE liability is limited to wearing apparel not to exceed One Hundred Dollars in value for a whole ticket and Fifty Dollars for a half ticket.

4th. ALTERATIONS. This ticket is void if coupons are detached from contract or if more than one destination is indicated or if any alterations or erasures are made hereon.

5th. REGULATIONS AND EXCHANGE. This ticket is subject to the rules and regulations of each line over which it reads, and may be exchanged in whole or in part for a ticket or check conforming to such rules and regulations.

6th. NON-MODIFICATION OF TERMS. No agent or employee has any power to alter, modify or waive any of the conditions of this contract.

7th. RESPONSIBILITY. In selling this ticket for passage over other lines and in checking baggage on it, the Pacific Railway & Navigation Company acts only as Agent and is not responsible beyond its own lines.

General Passenger Agent

Via CORVALLIS & EASTERN RAILROAD COMPANY.

One First Class Passage

YAQUINA, Ore.

TO

DESTINATION.

Subject to Conditions named in Contract.

| Baggage Checked |
| ★ Punch Here |
| If for Half ½ Punch Here |

Issued by **CORVALLIS & EASTERN R. R. CO.**

| Form NN-5 | Not Good if Detached. |

NNCo, C&E.

Via NEWPORT NAVIGATION COMPANY.

One First Class Passage

NEWPORT, Ore.

TO

YAQUINA, Ore.

Subject to Conditions named in Contract.

Destination_____

| Baggage Checked |
| ★ Punch Here |
| If for Half ½ Punch Here |

Issued by **CORVALLIS & EASTERN R. R. CO.**

| Form NN-5 | Not Good if Detached. |

NNCo, C&E.

The post office and the railroad station shared the same building in Niagra. Here the North Santiam River gushes violently through a narrow gorge, the fact behind the town's name. At one time promoters believed the site an excellent one for a paper mill and a hydroelectric development. The photo was taken in 1920.

Lillie Wilson, assistant postmaster, stands in the doorway of Thomas station in 1898. The building served as a post office as well.

The Mill City station was located in the basement of the hotel and post office, which can be seen at the right of this 1915 photograph.

Engineer Dick Casteel sits on the steamdome of the locomotive in Detroit in 1903. The station is to the left. Today the town seen here is under 100 feet of water in the center of the Detroit Dam.

CHAPTER 10

THE SUMPTER VALLEY
RAILWAY COMPANY

This rail line, affectionately called the "Stump Dodger" by its passengers, included a little more than eighty miles of narrow gauge track between Baker City and Prairie City. Gordon Steward relates, "A ride on the 'Stump Dodger' was full of bounce. In fact, it is told as truth that once when a section of smooth new rails was laid on the three-foot wide gauge, the ride became so calm that one passenger yelled, 'Jump for your lives. We're off the track'."

The Sumpter Valley Rail line was built by David C. Eccles of Utah in 1890. It reached Sumpter in 1897 and Prairie City in 1909. It was planned in the beginning to extend the line for a connection with the Nevada-California-Oregon Railroad, which was building northward from Reno, Nevada. But the connection never materialized. Cattlemen, prospectors, and lumbermen of eastern Oregon relied upon the SV for service to lumber mills along the line, mines at Sumpter, and cattle ranches in the Prairie City area. Piece by piece, the railroad was abandoned in the '30s, until one of Oregon's most picturesque lines was entirely gone.

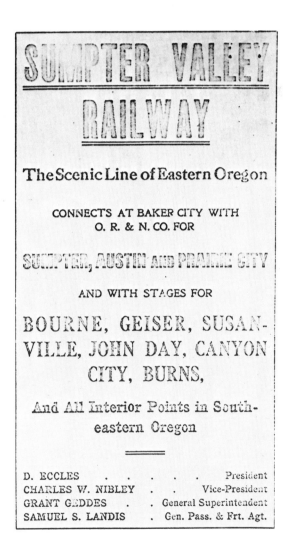

SUMPTER VALLEY
RAILWAY

The Scenic Line of Eastern Oregon

CONNECTS AT BAKER CITY WITH
O. R. & N. CO. FOR

SUMPTER, AUSTIN AND PRAIRIE CITY

AND WITH STAGES FOR

BOURNE, GEISER, SUSAN-
VILLE, JOHN DAY, CANYON
CITY, BURNS,

And All Interior Points in Southeastern Oregon

D. ECCLES . . . . . President
CHARLES W. NIBLEY . . Vice-President
GRANT GEDDES . . General Superintendent
SAMUEL S. LANDIS . Gen. Pass. & Frt. Agt.

SUMPTER VALLEY RAILWAY.

W. J. Eccles, President and
    General Manager, Baker, Ore.
D. I. Stoddard, Vice-Prest.,
              Baker, Ore.

A. S. Howe, Supt.,   Baker, Ore.
J. W. Pentney, Auditor,   „
Nichols, Hallock & Donald,
    Gen. Attorneys, Baker, Ore.

3	No. 1	Mls	*February*, 1931.	Elev.	4	No. 2
.....	*8 00 A M	0	lve...... **Baker**[1] ⊙..arr.	3437	.....	4 55 P M
.....	8 05 „	1.5	arr... South Baker⊙ lve.	3500	.....	4 50 „
.....	8 10 „	1.5	lve... South Baker ..arr.	3500	.....	4 50 „
.....	8 30 „	9.5	.... Salisbury ......⊙	3675	.....	— —
.....	8 50 „	16.2	.....Boulder Gorge...⊙	.....	.....	4 00 „
.....	9 10 „	22.5	........McEwen......⊙	4129	.....	3 55 „
.....	9 40 „	29.0	.... Sumpter......⊙	4420	.....	3 10 „
.....	10 15 „	34.7	.... Larch ....⊙	5090	.....	2 45 „
.....	10 45 „	43.4	........Whitney......⊙	4153	.....	2 00 „
.....	11 20 „	51.0	.... Tipton.......⊙	5090	.....	1 35 „
⊡	11 55 A M	59.2	arr...... Austin⊙ ...lve.	4106	⊡	12 50 „
P M	12 00 Noon	59.2	lve...... Austin .....arr.	4106	A M	12 45 „
*12 30	12 05 P M	60.2	.... Bates ....⊙	....	10 40	*12 40 P M
1 30	....	68.3	.... Dixie ....⊙	....	10 00	....
2 20	....	80.1	.... **Prairie**[2] ......⊙	3445	*9 00	....
P M	....	....	ARRIVE]	[LEAVE	A M	....

* Daily.   ⊡ Motor car.   ⊙ Telephone stations.   *Pacific time.*

Connections.—[1]With Oregon-Wash. R.R. & N. Co. [2]With stage lines for John Day, Canyon City, Burns and the great Harney Valley.

Mollie Irwin waits for the SV at what may be the smallest station known. Using the most common lumber grown in the area, the tiny station was built before there was such a phrase as "knotty pine."

Tipton Station awaits the train arrival, 1920

Ready to take off from Baker, 1930

Arrival of train at Sumpter, 1907

Prairie City, the end of the line, about 1910

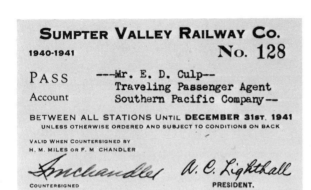

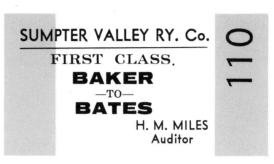

Somewhere along the Sumpter Valley line, about 1910

CHAPTER 11

MALHEUR VALLEY RAILWAY COMPANY (UP)

This railroad was built in 1907 from Malheur Junction to Vale, a distance of thirteen miles, by a group of promoters which included Stephen Carver. The line was constructed as a private venture, and, immediately after completion, they leased the trackage to the Oregon Short Line, a Union Pacific Subsidiary. Shortly after the track was extended to Brogan in 1910, both portions of the railroad were sold to the Oregon Washington Railway & Navigation Company, another Union Pacific subsidiary.

Stephen Carver, a railroad promoter well known in the annals of Oregon history, promoted the building of two other short lines there. All were sold shortly after completion to large public carriers.

Edward Henry Harriman of Union Pacific fame, who at this period also controlled the operation of the Southern Pacific, intended extending the MVRR through the Malheur canyon and across the central part of the state, making a connection with the SP at some point south of Eugene on the Cascade Line. From an operating standpoint, this would be an ideal route. Mr. Harriman had started this extension when the United States Supreme Court attacked the UP-SP consolidation as a combination in restraint of trade under the terms of the Sherman Anti-Trust Act of 1890. The directive really meant that the SP would be returned its independence from UP supervision. As a result of this decision, the proposed railroad through the Malheur Valley and the central part of the state was dropped.

This forest products line was built in 1926 from Telocaset on the Union Pacific Railroad to Pondosa, eleven miles away. The line was actually extended several miles beyond in a southeast direction into the foothills of the Wallowa's. A large mill was constructed at Pondosa—the "bull Buck's" name for Ponderosa Pine. Photo taken along the line of Big Creek & Telocaset Railway Company. (Photo by Henry R. Griffiths, 1948)

Right, The UMATILLA CENTRAL RAIL-ROAD COMPANY was fourteen miles of track built from Pilot Rock Junction (Reith) on the Union Pacific Railroad to the town of Pilot Rock. It was built by ORN and operated as a separate corporation. In 1910 the ORN included it as a part of their own line. This photograph shows the first train into Pilot Rock, December 16, 1907, with engineer "Dad" Moon at the throttle. *Below,* The Umatilla Central Railroad Company schedule.

Length of passing tracks in to clear and location of scales, water, fuel and turning stations.	WESTWARD. First Class.		DISTANCES FROM PILOT ROCK JCT.	STATIONS	STATION NUMBERS	EASTWARD. First Class.		
	41 Mixed Daily Ex. Sun.					42 Mixed Daily Ex. Sun.		
1305 TW	PM L 1.30		14.0	DR PILOT ROCK	AG14	AM A 10.30		
1500	f 1 50		6.0	8.0 SPARKS	AG6	f 9.55		
6980	2.05 PM A		0.0	6.0 R PILOT ROCK JCT.	A227	9.30 AM L		
	Daily Ex. Sun.			14.0		Daily Ex. Sun.		

This thirty mile public carrier line was built in 1929 from Condon through Kinzua and beyond in Gilliam County to handle forest products. Until 1952 the line operated "Goose," shown here, to handle passengers and mail. This Mack Rail Bus was formerly used on the Willamina & Grand Ronde Railroad.

ILWACO RAILWAY & STEAM
NAVIGATION COMPANY
RAILROAD (UP)

This railroad, built in 1888, operated from Megler to Nahcotta on Willapa Bay, a twenty-seven mile trip. Although the line was located in Washington, it depended almost entirely upon Oregon folk to keep it in operation. A trip down the Columbia River from Portland on one of the luxurious river boats, plus a rail trip over this small narrow gauge line to one of the north beaches, was the beginning of a wonderful vacation.

In the early days of the line, an editor of an Ilwaco newspaper prepared his own timetable for the line, much to the chagrin of the management.

Train Leaves

Ilwaco Dock .... When it gets ready

Arrives at

Nahcotta .... When it gets there

The line was purchased in 1900 by the Oregon Railway & Navigation Company and abandoned in 1930.

The arrival of the Oregon Railway & Navigation Company's T. J. Potter, the fastest riverboat on the Columbia River, at Megler, Washington. (Union Pacific photo)

Named after the Scottish poet, Burns is located in the heart of the Range country in Harney County. The railroad reached Burns in 1924, and this 1963 photo shows the station that was built shortly thereafter. Many refer to this area as the last outpost of the real Old West, where history is so young that a number still living can tell first hand of the settling of this country.

Oregon & Northwestern Railroad Co., 1955 at Summit, Oregon. This railroad is a fifty-two mile logging line operating from Burns on the Union Pacific Railroad to Seneca. The line is owned by Edward Hines Lumber Company.
(Photo by Henry R. Griffiths)

This station, photographed in 1960, is probably the outstanding architectural structure in this small town. It is an attractive two-story colonial dwelling, with the lower half built of stone. The upstairs affords living quarters for the Agent and his family. The town is the trade center of a large sheep-raising and wool region, but passenger service was discontinued here in the early '30s. The entire valley and surrounding range country were once owned by Henry Miller, one of the most important cattle barons in eastern Oregon.

THE COLUMBIA SOUTHERN RAILWAY

The Columbia Southern Railway Company was a seventy mile rail line built in 1897 from Biggs on the Columbia River to Shaniko, and was planned to run on to Prineville and into Central Oregon. Although Elmer Elm Lytle, a former Union Pacific employee, built the line, many believed that it was secretly financed by E. H. Harriman, president of the Union Pacific.

After reaching Shaniko, situated on a high plateau, the railroad engineers realized they had boxed themselves in. They found, finally, the Deschutes Canyon much more to their liking for building into central Oregon.

The OWR&N leased the line in 1906. Little by little, the line was dismantled until, in 1966, it was entirely gone.

Columbia Southern Railway Company

TIME TABLE

Effective 12:01 a. m., September 9, 1900

First Class	STATIONS	First Class
South Bound		North Bound
No. 2 DAILY PASSENGER		No. 1 DAILY PASSENGER
Leave P. M.		Arrive A. M.
1 34	BIGGS	11 25
1 59	Gibsons	11 00
2 14	Wasco	10 45
2 27	Klondyke	10 30
2 33	Summit	10 25
2 45	Hay Canyon Junction	10 15
2 48	McDonalds	10 12
3 00	DeMoss	10 00
3 09	Moro	9 50
3 19	Erskinville	9 39
3 44	Grass Valley	9 15
4 06	Bourbon	8 55
4 26	Kent	8 40
4 40	Wilcox	8 30
5 20	SHANIKO	8 00
Arrive P. M.		Leave A. M.

Daily Stage Line Connections

— TO —

ANTELOPE	CROSS KEYS	HAY CREEK
GRIZLEY	PRINEVILLE	CLARNO
FOSSIL	ASHWOOD	GRADE
MITCHELL	PAULINA	MOWRY
RILEY	PRICE	BURNS
SISTERS	PASLEY	SILVER LAKE
LAKEVIEW	LAMONTA	WARM SPRINGS
†ANTONE	†DAYVILLE	†JOHN DAY	†CANYON CITY

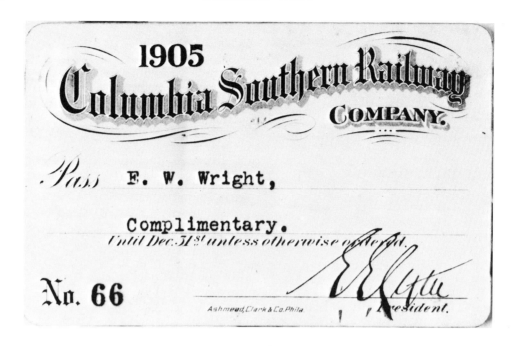

Wasco's station in 1905

THE GREAT SOUTHERN
RAILROAD

The Great Southern Railroad, built in 1904 by John Heimrich, was a forty mile long line running from the Dalles to Dufur and Friend. The train left Friend at 8 A.M., arriving at The Dalles in time to make the connection with the OR&N noon train with passengers, mail, and express. It arrived back in Friend that same evening. The line handled mainly wheat and some forest products. In 1936, the Wasco County Court sold the line for junk to cover unpaid taxes.

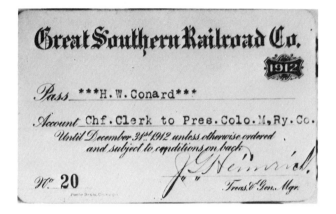

No. 1 Daily	Miles	STATIONS	No. 2 Daily
		GREAT SOUTHERN RAILROAD	
8.00	0	Lv THE DALLES Ar	3.45
f 8.10	3	..... Seuferts	f 3.26
f 8.27	5	..... Petersburg	f 3.16
8.42	10	..... Fairbanks	3.00
f 8.55	14	... Brookhouse ...	f 2.48
9.02	16	... Freebridge ...	2.41
f 9.08	18	..... Neabeck	f 2.35
9.20	21	..... Wrentham	2.19
f 9.30	24	..... Rice	f 2.07
9.44	27	..... Boyd	1.55
10.00	30	... Dufur ...	1.45
f10.20	35	..... Annalore	f 1.25
f10.32	38	..... Three Springs	f 1.13
10.45	41	Ar ..... Friend Lv	1.00

Dufur in 1907, one of the stops on the Great Southern

THE OREGON SHORT LINE (UP)

The Oregon Short Line, a Union Pacific subsidiary with 540 miles of track, was built in 1882 from Granger, Wyoming to Huntington, Oregon. Only fifteen miles of this trackage extends into Oregon. The line connected at Huntington with the OR&N on November 25, 1884.

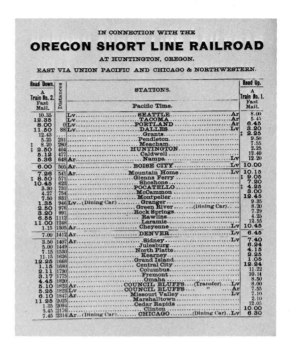

IN CONNECTION WITH THE

OREGON SHORT LINE RAILROAD

AT HUNTINGTON, OREGON.

EAST VIA UNION PACIFIC AND CHICAGO & NORTHWESTERN.

Road Down. A Train No. 2 Fast Mail.	Distances	STATIONS. Pacific Time.	Road Up. A Train No. 1 Fast Mail.
10.35		Lv........SEATTLE........Ar	8.00
12.35		Lv........TACOMA........Ar	5.45
8.00	0	Lv........PORTLAND........Ar	6.45
11.50	88	Lv........DALLES........Lv	3.20
12.43		........Grants........	2.25
5.25	231	........Pendleton........	9.50
8.20	280	........Meacham........	7.55
2.50	404	........HUNTINGTON........	2.25
5.12	477	........Caldwell........	12.40
5.36	648	Ar........Nampa........Lv	12.20
6.00	505	........BOISE CITY........Lv	10.00
7.25	541	Ar........Mountain Home........Lv	10.15
8.50	571	........Glenns Ferry........	9.05
10.45	623	........Shoshone........	7.20
3.30	731	........POCATELLO........	4.25
4.27	754	........McCammon........	3.00
7.50	831	........Montpelier........	12.45
1.35	946	Lv..(Dining Car)..Granger........	9.35
2.50	976	........Green River........(Dining Car)..	8.20
3.20	991	........Rock Springs........	7.29
6.55	1112	........Rawlins........	4.25
11.00	1246	........Laramie........	12.55
1.15	1305	Ar........Cheyenne........Lv	10.45
7.00	1412	Ar........DENVER........Lv	6.45
3.50	1407	Ar........Sidney........Lv	7.40
5.00	1449	........Julesburg........	6.24
7.15	1530	........North Platte........	4.15
11.15	1626	........Kearney........	2.25
12.25	1668	........Grand Island........	1.05
1.15	1680	........Central City........	12.24
2.11	1730	........Columbus........	11.22
3.17	1773	........Fremont........	10.14
4.45	1820	........Omaha........	8.50
5.10	1823	Ar........COUNCIL BLUFFS........(Transfer)....Lv	8.00
5.26	1823	Lv " COUNCIL BLUFFS " Ar	7.55
6.10	1847	........Missouri Valley........Lv	7.10
11.25	2025	........Marshalltown........	2.10
1.35	2094	........Cedar Rapids........	12.05
3.45	2176	........Clinton........	10.00
7.45	2314	Ar..(Dining Car)..CHICAGO........(Dining Car)..Lv	6.30

Station and station park in Ontario in 1920

MOUNT HOOD RAILROAD CO.
(UP)

The Mount Hood Railroad, built by the Eccles people of Utah, is a twenty-two mile line that climbs 1,689 feet from Hood River to Parkdale, the end of the line. The big sawmill at Dee became the railroad's first large industrial operation when the road reached there in 1906. Construction was continued to Parkdale in 1910. Today the line handles many perishables, including the famous Hood River apples. It was purchased by the Union Pacific in October 1968.

MT. HOOD RAILROAD CO.

Employee's Time Table No. 44
Taking Effect Sunday, April 2, 1933, 12:01 A. M.

SOUTHBOUND				NORTHBOUND		
*No. 1	†No. 3	‡No. 5		‡No. 6	†No. 4	*No. 2
A. M.	A. M.	P. M.	Lv. Ar.	P. M.	A. M.	P. M.
9:00	8:00	1:30	____Hood River____	4:00	10:30	4:15
9:10	8:03	1:33	____Powerdale____	3:56	10:26	4:10
9:25	8:13	1:43	____Switchback____	3:48	10:20	4:00
9:50	8:21	1:51	____Pine Grove____	3:38	10:10	3:46
10:06	8:24	1:54	_____Mohr_____	3:34	10:06	3:39
10:32	8:31	1:59	_____Odell_____	3:30	10:02	3:30
10:39	8:37	2:05	____Summit____	3:26	9:56	3:17
10:50	8:42	2:10	____Holstein____	3:20	9:50	2:57
10:55	8:45	2:13	_____Winans____	3:17	9:47	2:50
11:00			Ar.____Dee____Lv.	3:15	9:45	2:45
11:20	8:50	2:20	Lv.____Dee____Ar.			12:55
11:30	8:55	2:25	____Trout Creek____	3:08	9:38	12:50
11:50	9:05	2:35	____Woodworth____	3:03	9:33	12:40
12:00	9:10	2:40	Ar.__Parkdale _Lv.	3:00	9:30	12:30

†Motors No. 3 and No. 4 Daily.   *Steam Train Daily Except Sunday.
‡Motors No. 5 and No. 6 Daily Except Sunday.
PACIFIC TIME

Numbers 4 and 5 connect with O. W. R. R. & N. train Number 20.

Numbers 3, 4, 5 and 6, Motors, have right over Numbers 1 and 2. Steam trains will clear time of motor cars at all meeting and passing points five (5) minutes. Steam trains will occupy main line at meeting and passing points, but will permit motors to pass without delay. Motor cars will approach sidings and stations cautiously, expecting to find main line occupied.

Owing to limited space on motor cars, all trunks and heavy baggage will be handled on steam trains, either in advance or following the passengers.

The railroad station in Parkdale (building at right), photographed in 1920, looks like someone's home. Indeed, a portion of the building is used as a hotel. The background including beautiful Mt. Hood, is very near and very real.

CHAPTER 12

PACIFIC RAILWAY & NAVIGATION COMPANY (SP)

The Pacific Railway & Navigation Company was incorporated in 1905 and comprises ninety-one miles of curves, high trestles, and tunnels that begin at Hillsboro, cross the Coast range, explore many of the beaches, and end at the city of Tillamook.

In the early years of the century, the Southern Pacific was owned and controlled by Edward Harriman of the Union Pacific Railroad. James J. Hill, the empire builder of the Great Northern Railway, considered purchasing the Astoria & Columbia River Railroad running from Portland to Seaside. It was rumored that Hill would continue building from Seaside southward, extending his railroad along the entire Oregon coast to a connection with a California line.

Harriman put Elmer Elm Lytle in charge of building the PR&N, with instructions to center his line through much of the coastal area. This plan would make it difficult for the construction of a rival railroad in the event that Hill decided to build on down the coast.

This decision meant that the shortest route between Hillsboro and Tillamook

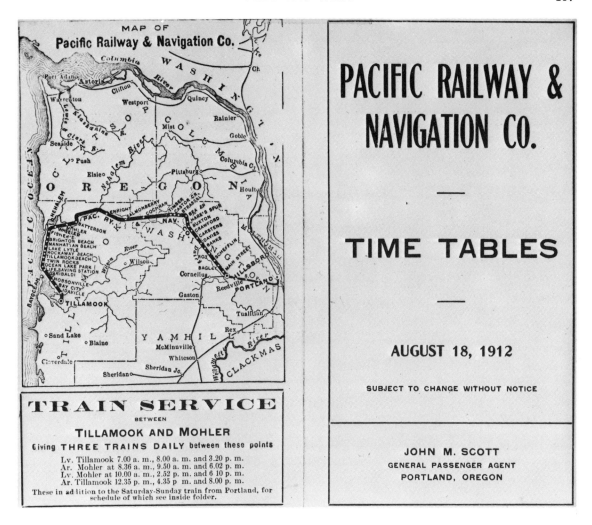

PACIFIC RAILWAY &
NAVIGATION CO.

—

TIME TABLES

—

AUGUST 18, 1912

SUBJECT TO CHANGE WITHOUT NOTICE

JOHN M. SCOTT
GENERAL PASSENGER AGENT
PORTLAND, OREGON

TRAIN SERVICE
BETWEEN
TILLAMOOK AND MOHLER
Giving THREE TRAINS DAILY between these points

Lv. Tillamook 7.00 a. m., 8.00 a. m. and 3.20 p. m.
Ar. Mohler at 8.36 a. m., 9.50 a. m. and 6.02 p. m.
Lv. Mohler at 10.00 a. m., 2.52 p. m. and 6 10 p. m.
Ar. Tillamook 12.35 p. m., 4.35 p m. and 8.00 p. m.
These in addition to the Saturday-Sunday train from Portland, for
schedule of which see inside folder.

was not selected as the roadbed for the PR&N. Construction was begun at both ends of the line in 1906-7. But the depression of 1907 set the building program back, and the line was not opened until October 1911. Whatever the reason, Jim Hill and the A&CRR made no attempt to build down the coast.

"The trip from Portland to the Tillamook County Beach resorts presents an ever-changing pano-
rama of scenic charm. We pass through Beaverton, Reedville and Hillsboro, thriving towns which
recall the early days of Oregon's history. Soon the foot-hills are entered and on both sides of the
track the wild currant bravely flings to the breeze its banner of bloom. At Timber station, located
in the heart of the great woods and near the summit of the Coast Range, an artistic station of logs
    shows that timber is the principal product of the section."—from PR&N advertising booklet.

Five miles west of Timber, Cochran rests on a summit of the Coast Range at 1,811 feet. In 1918,
Cochran's agent, William B. Johnstone, leans against the small station. In the background is the
                                Wheeler Lumber Company.

SP Train No. 142, the Tillamook Flyer, enroute to Portland: Lv. Tillamook—7:40 A.M.; Ar. Salmonberry—9:47 A.M.; Ar. Portland—1:47 P.M. The burned area behind the station in this 1917 photo illustrates the plague of Oregon for generations. Oregon's most terrible forest fire, The Tillamook Burn, occurred August 1933, with fire consuming thirteen billion board feet of timber. As one man described it, "The heart of the greatest timber producing state in the nation burned out in fourteen days."

Below, Advertising schedules for the popular Tillamook beaches

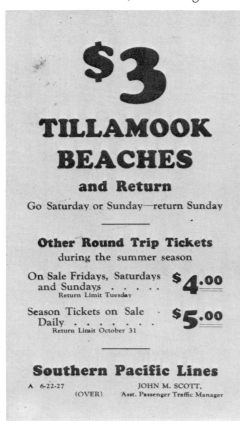

Lake Lytle had one of the choice beaches in Tillamook County. The lake and the hotel, seen in these 1915 photos, were named after Elmer Elm Lytle, president and builder of the Pacific Railway & Navigation Company. The rustic log cabin was located at what is today the center of the coast highway.

Beach trains became a great favorite with the public. The trains carried passsengers to within a block of the Pacific Ocean. Cottages and tent cities were close by for the tourists' convenience. In this 1916 photo, the Rockaway station is crowded with expectant people, awaiting the biggest event of the day, the arrival of the flyer from Portland.

Train No. 142, the Tillamook Flyer, headed for Portland in 1922. It left Tillamook at 7:20 A.M. and arrived at Garibaldi at 7:55, proceeding on to Portland, arriving at 1:55 P.M.

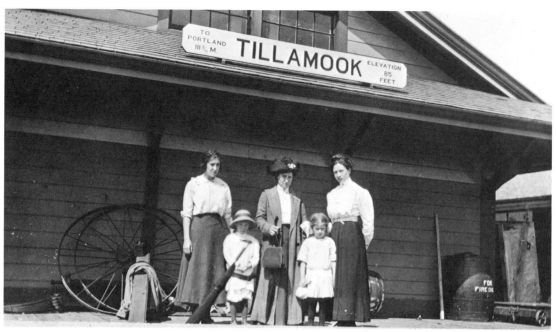

"Land of cheese, trees, and ocean breeze"

"The Tillamook beaches—delightful—restful. . . . Portland's nearest seaside resorts are those located on Tillamook County beaches. Draw a line due west from Portland and it will meet the Pacific Ocean in the heart of the Tillamook County beach resort district."—from SP advertising booklet.

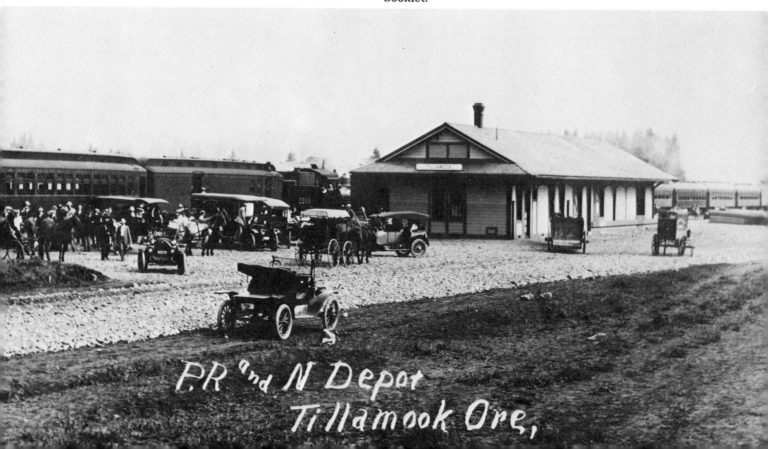

P.R. and N Depot
Tillamook Ore,

Wheeler station, with the Wheeler Lumber Company in the background, about 1920

The station serving the beach resort at Barview, in 1916

Those detraining at Bay City were usually enroute to Bay Ocean. Located across Tillamook Bay and reached by a motor launch, Bay Ocean was one of the deluxe coastal playgrounds of the Pacific coast. Sometime after this 1914 photograph was taken, a storm devastated Bay Ocean, washing many of the buildings out to sea.

CHAPTER 13

THE ASTORIA-SEASIDE LINE
(BN)

The 122 miles of trackage that run from Portland to Seaside were constructed by three different and unrelated groups. At one time, each portion of the line had its own identity. Today they have merged as a part of the Burlington Northern Railway.

In 1883 the Northern Pacific Railway Company, in laying trackage between Portland and Tacoma or Seattle, built forty miles of rail from Portland to Goble, a station located along the banks of the Columbia River. From Goble the entire train was ferried across the river to Kalama, Washington. In 1911 the NP discontinued using this trackage as a main line, but the company has always retained ownership.

In 1889 a group of businessmen planned a railroad from Astoria to Hills-

boro, which they would call the Astoria & South Coast Railroad. Construction was started at Hillsboro and at Warrenton. Work on the Hillsboro portion was soon stopped for lack of finances, but the Clatsop County portion was built from

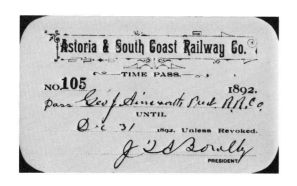

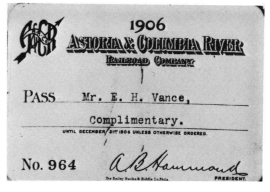

ASTORIA & COLUMBIA RIVER RAILROAD

PORTLAND-ASTORIA-SEASIDE—MAIN LINE

WESTBOUND—READ DOWN   EASTBOUND—READ UP

No.7 Daily	No.5 Daily	No.11 Sat only	No.9 Daily	No.3 Daily	No.1 Daily	Miles	TABLE No.7	No.2 Daily	No.10 Daily	No.4 Daily	No.12 Sa. only	No.6 Daily	No.8 Daily
5 45	1 15	2 30	6 30	9 20	8 00	0.0	Lv..Portland§..Ar	12 06	10 00	10 15	12 30	9 40	f 5 00
5 53	f 1 30					6.0	..Claremont..					f 9 23	f 4 45
6 02	1 33				8 17	7.2	..Linnton§..	11 48	9 43			9 20	f 4 42
f 6 13	f 1 42			8 22		11.5	..Burlington..		f 9 32			f 9 12	f 4 30
6 15	1 44			8 25		12.5	..Holbrook..		f 9 30			9 10	4 30
f 6 23	f 1 53					17.3	..Johnsons..					f 9 03	f 4 20
6 30	2 00			8 40		19.8	..Scappoose§..	11 23	9 15			8 57	4 13
f 6 32	f 2 02			8 42		20.8	..Honeymans..					f 8 55	f 4 11
6 42	2 09			8 48		24.2	..Warren..		f 9 05			8 48	4 03
6 49	2 16			8 55		27.5	..Houlton§..	11 02	8 52			8 32	3 55
6 58	2 24			9 02		31.2	..Columbia..		f 8 49			8 25	3 47
7 03	2 30			9 07		33.7	..Deer Island..		f 8 43			8 20	3 42
f 7 08	f 2 33					35.7	..Tide Creek..					f 8 15	f 3 38
f 7 12	f 2 37					37.2	..Charlton..					f 8 12	f 3 34
f 7 14	f 2 40			9 17		38.4	..Nehalem Jct...					f 8 10	f 3 32
7 18	2 42	3 30	7 34	9 19		39.4	..Goble§..	10 43	8 31			8 08	3 30
f 7 23	f 2 48			9 25		42.8	..Prescott..		f 8 24			f 7 57	f 3 22
f 7 25	f 2 50					43.8	..Oasis..					f 7 55	f 3 20
7 30	2 55	3 40	7 45	10 30	9 32	45.8	Ar..Rainier§..Lv	10 30	8 17	9 01	11 16	7 50	3 15
			7 55		f 9 43	51.5	..Rinearson..	f10 18	f 8 05				
			7 59			53.0	..Downings..	f10 14					
			8 00		f 9 48	53.5	..Pyramid..	f10 13	f 8 00				
			8 07		f 9 53	55.9	..Mayger..	f10 08	7 55				
			8 20		f 10 00	59.3	..Quincy..	f10 00	7 46				
			8 23		f 10 03	60.5	..Inglis..	f 9 57	f 7 42				
			8 30		10 07	62.3	..Clatskanie§..	f 9 45	7 38				
			8 33		f 10 10	63.6	..Palm..	f 9 42	f 7 35				
			8 39		f 10 19	66.6	..Marshland..	9 42	f 7 28				
			8 44		f 10 25	69.2	..Woods Landing..	f 9 36	f 7 22				
			8 47		f 10 28	70.2	..Ross Landing..	f 9 33	f 7 19				
			8 49		f 10 30	71.2	..Westport..	9 31	7 17				
			8 57		f 10 42	75.2	..Bugby..	f 9 22	f 7 08				
			9 03		f 10 47	77.2	..Parsons..	f 9 17	f 7 02				
			9 10		f 10 51	78.7	..Clifton..	f 9 13	f 7 00				
			9 15		f 10 58	81.7	..Aldrich Point..	f 9 06	f 6 53				
			9 20		f 11 07	84.6	..Blind Slough..	8 58	f 6 45				
			9 28		f 11 12	86.6	..Knappa..	8 53	f 6 40				
			9 30		f 11 20	90.3	..Svenson..	8 43	f 6 32				
			9 35		f 11 22	91.3	..Burnside..	8 40	f 6 29				
			9 38		f 11 29	94.0	..Fern Hill..	8 35	f 6 23				
					f 11 33	95.4	..John Day..	8 32	f 6 20				
			9 42		f 11 37	96.8	..Tongue Point..	8 28	6 18				
			9 43		f 11 38	97.3	..Hume..	f 8 27	f 6 17				
			9 50		11 45	99.8	Ar..Astoria§..Lv	8 20	6 10	7 20	9 40		

For additional trains between Astoria and Warrenton see Table No. 10. Ft. Stevens time, Table No. 10.

Clatsop Beach (Astoria–Holladay)

No.17 Daily	No.15 Daily	No.13 Daily	No.11	No.9	No.3	No.1	Miles	TABLE No.7	No.2 Daily	No.10 Daily	No.4 Daily	No.12 Sa. only	No.14 Daily	No.16 Daily	No.18 Daily
6 10	3 00	8 30	5 15	9 50	12 10	11 45	99.8	Lv..Astoria§..Ar	8 15	5 50	7 20	9 35	10 15	4 45	11 00
f 6 22	f 3 15	f 8 42	5 20	9 55	12 10	11 50	104.2	..Sunnymead..					f10 00	f 4 30	f10 45
f 6 22	f 3 15	f 8 42					104.3	..Meriwether..					f 9 59	f 4 29	f10 44
6 28	3 20	8 45	5 35	10 15	12 25	12 40	105.7	..Warrenton§..	7 55	5 35	7 05	9 20	9 55	4 25	10 40
f 6 31	f 3 23	8 48	f 5 38	f10 18	f12 29	f12 13	107.0	..Skipanon (a)..	f 7 52	f 5 30	f 7 01	f 9 16	f 9 52	f 4 22	10 12
6 35	3 28	8 51	5 42	10 21	12 33	12 16	108.4	..Morrison (b)..	7 49	5 27	6 57	9 12	9 49	4 19	10 10
f 6 39	f 3 29	f 8 53	5 45	f10 24	12 37	f12 18	109.8	..Glenwood...	f 7 46	5 24	6 53	f 9 08	9 46	4 16	10 07
f 6 41	f 3 31	f 8 55	f 5 48	f10 26	f12 39	f12 20	110.6	..Carnahan (c)..	f 7 44	f 5 22	6 52	f 9 07	f 9 44	4 14	10 05
f 6 48	f 3 34	f 9 03	5 51	10 29	12 43	12 23	112.1	..West..	7 41	5 19	6 48	9 03	9 41	4 11	10 02
f 6 50	f 3 37	f 9 05	5 54	10 32	12 45	12 25	113.2	..Clatsop..	7 38	5 16	6 46	9 01	9 38	4 08	9 59
f 6 53	f 3 39	f 9 07	5 58	10 34	12 48	12 27	114.5	..Butterfield..	f 7 36	5 13	6 44	8 59	9 36	4 06	9 56
6 55	3 41	9 09	5 58	10 36	12 51	12 30	115.7	..Gearhart§(d)..	7 34	5 10	6 42	8 56	9 34	4 04	9 53
f 6 57	f 3 43	9 11	6 00	10 38	12 54	12 34	116.8	..Wahanna..	f 7 32	5 05	6 39	8 52	9 32	4 02	9 50
f 6 58	f 3 44	f 9 13	6 02	10 39	12 56	12 37	117.5	..Necanicum..	f 7 31	5 03	6 37	8 51	9 31	4 01	9 47
7 00	3 45	9 15	6 05	10 40	1 00	12 40	118.1	..Seaside§..	7 30	5 00	6 35	8 50	9 30	4 00	9 45
7 05	3 50	9 20	6 10	10 45	1 10	12 50	119.1	Ar..Holladay.Lv	7 20	4 50	6 25	8 40	9 25	3 55	9 35

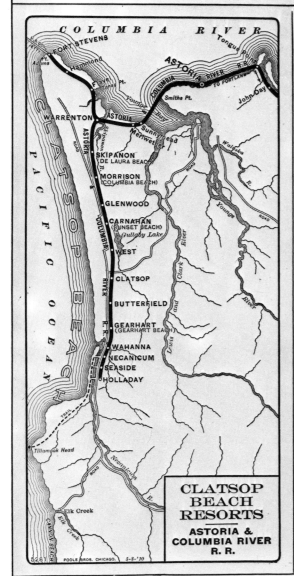

Andrew Benoni Hammond's A&CR Railroad served Astoria and the rugged and beautiful Clatsop Beach area on the Pacific.

Necanicum Station, Seaside, Oreg.   Woodfield, Photo.

The first railroad station in Seaside, built about 1893, was constructed on the west side of the Necanicum River, only a few hundred yards from the ocean. One of the railroad trestles began sinking into the river, and the line was forced to relocate. The new station was built on the east side of the Necanicum. This photo shows the Necanicum Inn as it looked about 1912. It was believed to be the former Astoria & South Coast Railroad station that had once been located on the west side of the river.

Young's Bay to Seaside. In a short while, the line changed its name to the Seashore Road Company, which ran from Astoria to Seaside. But in 1897, Andrew Benoni Hammond purchased the railroad and once again renamed it, calling it the Astoria & Columbia River Railroad. Hammond added to the line from Astoria, until he had made a connection with the NP at Goble. The first through train from Portland to the coast over the Seaside line ran in 1898.

Below, The station on the east side of the Necanicum, in 1910. "The Daddy Train" is nearly ready to roll on a Sunday afternoon to take the menfolk the 118 miles back to the business world in Portland. They would return late the next Saturday afternoon, the high point of the week for families vacationing at Seaside.

ASTORIA LINE

..The Scenic Seacoast Route..

SAFE, SWIFT AND SURE

Parlor Car of Astoria & Columbia River Railroad

2--TRAINS DAILY--2

=== ALL RAIL ===

From Union Depot, Portland, to the Sea

NO DELAYS NO TRANSFERS

A&CR No. 17 arrives in Astoria from Portland, met by the Parker House bus. The station is a two-story wooden structure built in 1898, the same year the first through train arrived from Portland. The photo was taken March 17, 1905.

The Spokane, Portland & Seattle Railroad Company station and wharf facilities

FLAVEL, COLUMBIA RIVER
Docking Point of S. S. Great Northern and Northern Pacific Where Connection is Made With North Bank Trains

FLAVEL

1915 was a big year: The Panama Canal opened, allowing ships to pass from one ocean to another; San Francisco celebrated the Panama-Pacific Exposition; and the Pacific Northwest was given a new deluxe travel route from Portland to San Francisco. The Great Northern and Northern Pacific Railways built two sister ships, each costing some three million dollars, for service to California. These luxuriously equipped ships could make the trip from Flavel to San Francisco in twenty-six hours.

This was a new and effective travel plan. A first-class round trip rail ticket from Chicago to San Francisco cost $90.00 (Pullman charges extra). After reaching Portland via NP or GN, one transferred to SP for the last leg of the trip. The same rail ticket entitled the holder to ship service from Flavel to San Francisco, without any additional charge for berth and meals at sea. One could then return to Portland by ship or rail. It was a good buy that was well patronized by the traveling public.

Gearhart in 1910, on the line a few miles north of Seaside

This 1910 photograph shows a train leaving Warren, Oregon, headed for Astoria

Hammond in 1910, located in the northernmost area of the Clatsop beach district on the A&CR

Camp One, headquarters for the P&S-W

THE PORTLAND &
SOUTHWESTERN RAILROAD

The P&SW was an eleven-mile public carrier and logging railroad built around 1911 and operated from Johnson's Landing on the Willamette Slough of the Columbia River, a half mile from the city of Scappoose. To serve the logging operations, the line extended back into the woods.

The Astoria train carried a through coach from Portland each Sunday to Scappoose, and from there the car was carried over the P&SW. The coach returned to Scappoose each evening for connection with the returning train to Portland. The headquarters of the line were at a point known as Camp One.

The through coach from Portland attached to a P&S-W locomotive, somewhere along the line

CHAPTER 14

THE OREGON TRUNK RAILWAY
VERSUS THE DESCHUTES
RAILROAD

James J. Hill of the Great Northern Railway and Edward H. Harriman of the Union Pacific simultaneously decided in 1909 to invade the Deschutes Canyon, with the intention of gaining access to central Oregon. Hill was to call his line the Oregon Trunk, while Harriman had dubbed his the Deschutes Railroad. Millions were to be spent and wasted on the building of these two railroads only to gratify a grudge fight between the two tycoons. Neither would allow the other the advantage.

Hill's men approached the canyon from one side while Harriman's worked to the other, with the swift Deschutes River flowing between. After considerable trackage had been constructed, the two discovered their folly and agreed to utilize the Oregon Trunk tracks, allowing each a joint operation through the canyon. The seventy miles of Harriman's track were to be abandoned.

The Oregon Trunk came to comprise 150 miles of trackage extending from the Columbia River on Oregon's northern border to Bend (see map). Each railroad constructed its own stations. The Harriman influence can be seen in the barn-like two-story structures, while the Hill interests built a low, one-story, rambling type of building.

OREGON TRUNK RY.

Read down   **Read up**

No. 5 Oregon Passenger Daily	No. 2 Inland Empire Express Daily	Miles	Spokane, Portland & Seattle Ry. May 18, 1912	No. 7 Oregon Passenger Daily	No. 1 Inland Empire Express Daily
8 20	9 55	0.0	Lv.............**Portland†**.........Ar.	5 30	7 45
8 43	f10 12	7.0	.............St. Johns†	5 06	f 7 20
8 56	10 21	10.0	.............**Vancouver†**	4 55	7 10
9 27	.....	24.4	.............Camas†	4 20	.....
9 35	.....	27.6	.............Washougal†	4 12	.....
10 34	.....	53.8	.............Stevenson†	3 13	f 5 55
11 17	.....	72.6	.............Underwood	2 30	.....
11 25	12 04	75.6	.............White Salmon†	2 22	5 18
11 48	12 24	85.3	.............**Lyle†**	2 00	4 57
12 08	f12 39	94.0	.............Granddalles†	1 41	f 4 41
12 40	1 00	106.1	Ar.............**Fallbridge†**.........Lv.	1 15	4 20

No. 102 Daily		Oregon Trunk Ry. May 18, 1912	No. 101 Daily
1 10	106.1	Lv.............**Fallbridge†**.........Ar.	§¶12 55
1 27	111.3	.............Moody†	12 38
f 1 40	117.0	.............Kloan	f12 26
f 1 55	123.6	.............Lockit	f12 12
f 2 15	131.1	.............Dyke	f11 53
f 2 25	136.0	.............Sinamox†	f11 44
f 2 46	145.5	.............Oakbrook	f11 23
f 3 05	153.2	.............Sherar†	f11 05
f 3 12	156.1	.............Tuskan	f10 58
3 22	161.0	.............Maupin†	10 48
f 3 42	169.4	.............Nena	f10 29
f 3 50	173.1	.............Frieda	f10 20
f 4 04	179.2	.............Nathan	f10 07
4 08	181.0	.............North Junction†	10 02
f 4 18	185.8	.............Kaskela	f 9 52
f 4 28	189.6	.............Jersey	f 9 42
4 32	191.4	.............South Junction†	9 38
f 4 39	194.3	.............Coleman	f 9 32
4 55	201.4	.............Mecca†	9 15
f 5 09	206.3	.............Vanora	f 9 04
f 5 21	210.5	.............Pelton	f 8 54
5 38	216.7	.............Madras†	8 40
¶ 5 50	220.8	Ar.............Metolius†.........Lv.	8 30
¶ 6 20	220.8	Lv.............Metolius†.........Ar.	8 22
6 35	225.6	.............Culver†	8 09
f 6 53	232.5	.............Opal City	f 7 51
f 7 15	240.2	.............Terrebonne	f 7 30
7 30	245.6	.............Redmond†	7 15
7 55	254.7	.............Deschutes†	6 50
8 15	262.1	Ar.............**Bend**.........Lv.	6 30

Light faced figures denote A. M. time. **Dark faced figures denote P. M. time.** f Stop on signal. †Telegraph. ¶Meals. §Connection between O. T. train No. 101 and S. P. & S. train No. 2 for Spokane and east. For S. P. & S. schedule see Page 2.

EQUIPMENT

Trains Nos. 6-102 and 101-7 carry first class coaches and smoking cars between Portland and Bend.

Trains Nos. 2 and 1 carry observation parlor cars, sleeping cars, dining cars, first class coaches and smoking cars between Portland and Fallbridge.

STAGES TO INTERIOR OREGON POINTS

Horse stages and autos leave points given below and charge the passenger fares shown below.

In most cases departures are on arrival of trains.

This information is from direct sources, but the Railway is not responsible for deviation therefrom.

FROM → TO ↓	MAUPIN Horse	CULVER Horse	REDMOND Horse	REDMOND Auto	BEND Horse	BEND Auto
Lamonta		$1.25				
Prineville		2.50	$2.00	3.00		
Post		7.50	4.50			
Paulina		10.50	7.50			
Fife		10.50	9.50			
Riley		10.75	11.00			
La Pine					$3.00	5.00
Fremont					6.25	10.00
Crescent					5.00	10.00
Ft. Rock					6.50	12.00
Silver Lake					9.00	15.00
Burns		12.50	12.00			20.00
Paisley					15.00	25.00
Lakeview					19.00	
Victor	$ .50					
Wapinitia	1.00					

One of the first public timetables used on the OREGON TRUNK. The map shows track constructed by Harriman and Hill on opposite sides of the Deschutes River. Through mutual agreement, Hill's OT tracks were used while Harriman abandoned his.

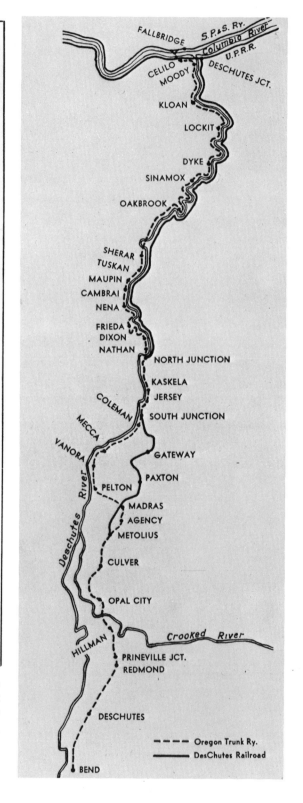

SPOKANE, PORTLAND & SEATTLE RY.
OREGON TRUNK RAILWAY

1913   No. E3166

Pass   ---Mr. R. E. White---
Account   Dispatcher
         Spokane, Portland & Seattle Ry
Between All Stations
Until   December 31,   1913   (Unless otherwise ordered and)
                                   (Subject to conditions on back.)

VALID WHEN COUNTERSIGNED BY F. A. PEIL

COUNTERSIGNED BY

                                                        President

---

Central Oregon
Redmond and Bend

Reached via the Deschutes Branch

Oregon-Washington Railroad & Nav. Co.

Through Car Service Between Portland and Bend

Auto and regular stage conections to La Pine, Fort Rock, Silver Lake, Prineville, Burns, Klamath Falls and other inland towns.

The Direct, Quick and Natural Route

For further information, call on any O.-W. R. & N. agent, or address

WM. McMURRAY
Gen'l Passenger Agt.   PORTLAND, ORE.

DAILY TRAIN SCHEDULE

Lv. Portland....7:50 & 10:00 a.m.	Lv. Bend .... 6:30 a.m.
Lv. The Dalles........12:40 p.m.	Lv. Redmond .... 7:21 a.m.
Lv. Deschutes Jct...... 1:30 p.m.	Lv. Opal City .... 8:00 a.m.
Ar. Madras .... 5:45 p.m.	Lv. Metolius .... 8:30 a.m.
Ar. Metolius .... 6:00 p.m.	Lv. Madras .... 8:45 a.m.
Ar. Opal City......... 7:06 p.m.	Ar. Deschutes Jct..... 1:05 p.m.
Ar. Redmond .... 7:45 p.m.	Ar. The Dalles .... 1:55 p.m.
Ar. Bend .... 8:35 p.m.	Ar. Portland .... 5:45 p.m.

(December 1911)

Bend in 1913 shortly after the new station (left) was opened

CHAPTER 15

THE CITY OF PRINEVILLE
RAILROAD

The City of Prineville Railroad is a nineteen-mile line owned and operated by the citizens of the town of Prineville. It was started in 1916 when the Oregon Trunk line, with trains operated by the Harriman and Hill interests, bypassed Prineville on their way from the Columbia to Redmond and Bend in central Oregon.

The local citizens cried out that "no blankety-blank big-time railroad was going to keep Prineville off the map," especially when doing so at that time would leave one of the biggest stands of timber in the country untouched. With no time to waste, a bond issue was voted by the townfolk and the railroad was constructed from Prineville to a connection with the Oregon Trunk line.

Today there are several large lumber mills in Prineville, all shipping their lading into the eastern transcontinental territory. The City of Prineville Railroad is a fully accredited public carrier line and, as the originating carrier on all freight moving from their city, receives a healthy percentage of the through freight rate.

The arrival of the train at Prineville, 1930

The City of Prineville Railway station, 1960

KLAMATH FALLS

James J. Hill, the empire builder, had tried several times to build a profitable railroad connection from his Great Northern tracks into California. In the Oregon Trunk, completed to Bend in 1911, he believed he saw the answer. It was natural that this line should tap some of western Oregon's larger cities and proceed right into California.

Since many of the points he hoped to reach were already served by Southern Pacific, he was eventually able to effect an agreement with the SP for trackage rights over seventy-four miles of its recently completed Natron cut-off from Chemult to Klamath Falls. So trackage was constructed from Bend to Chemult. When the GN ran its first train into Klamath Falls on May 10, 1928, it had extended its line 295 miles south from the Columbia River to within fifteen miles of the California state line.

Klamath Falls

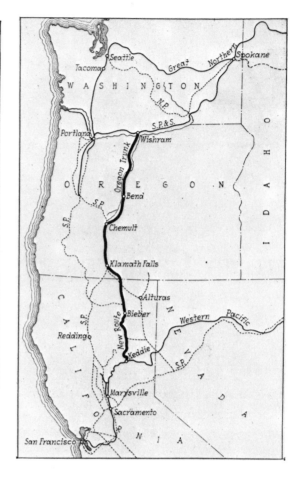

WISHRAM AND BEND OREGON TRUNK RY.			
Read Down			*Read Up*
102 Ex. Mon.	Mls	Table Pacific Time 82	103 Ex. Sun.
x12 30	0	Lv Wishram...Ar	x 3 55
f12 43	6	" Moody...... "	f 3 35
f 1 10	18	" Lockit....... "	f 2 58
f 1 27	26	" Dike........ "	f 2 31
f 2 29	51	" Tuskan...... "	f 1 33
2 41	55	" Maupin..... "	1 23
f 3 09	64	" Nena....... "	f12 55
f 3 20	68	" Frieda...... "	f12 44
f 3 39	74	" Nathan...... "	f12 26
3 44	75	" North Jct.... "	12 19
f 3 58	80	" Kaskela..... "	f12 05
f 4 10	84	" Jersey...... "	f11 57
4 15	86	" South Jct.... "	11 52
f 4 30	88	" Truman..... "	f11 38
f 4 40	94	" Gateway.... "	11 30
f 4 55	100	" Paxton...... "	f11 15
5 15	105	" Madras..... "	11 00
5 40	110	" Metolius..... "	10 45
x 5 54	115	" Culver...... "	10 33
f 6 16	122	" Opal City.... "	f10 15
f 6 40	129	" Terrebonne.. "	9 55
6 50	132	" Prineville Jct.. "	9 47
6 58	135	" Redmond.... "	9 45
f 7 25	144	" Deschutes... "	f 9 15
7 40	151	Ar Bend 83.....Lv	x 8 55

x—On Sundays train 310 leaves Wishram at 11:30 pm and arrives at Bend at 7:10 am Monday. Train 311 leaves Bend at 4:30 pm Sundays and arrives at Wishram at 11:00 pm. Intermediate time in both directions is changed accordingly.

f—Flag Stop.

BEND, KLAMATH FALLS, BIEBER & SAN FRANCISCO			
387 Mixed Daily	Mls	Table Pacific Time 83	386 Mixed Daily
		See Note.	
7 30	0	Lv Bend........Ar	1 30
f 8 50	13	" Lava......... "	f 2 37
8 55	15	" Lava Jct..... "	2 27
f 9 24	24	" Stearns...... "	f 1 45
f 9 40	32	" La Pine..... "	f 1 25
f 9 57	39	" Beal........ "	f12 55
f10 13	45	" Fremont..... "	f12 34
f10 28	52	" Crescent..... "	f12 11
f10 45	61	" Carroll...... "	f11 45
11 18	68	" Chemult..... "	f11 18
f 1 25	114	" Chiloquin.... "	f 9 11
f 2 05	131	" Algoma...... "	f 8 37
2 30	145	Ar Klamath Falls Lv	8 10
2 35	145	Lv Klamath Falls Ar	5 15
7 00	145	" So. Klamath... "	5 05
f 7 32	159	" Merrill....... "	f 4 30
f 7 55	169	" Malin....... "	f 4 10
f 8 15	178	" Stronghold.... "	f 3 40
8 45	188	" Mammoth.... "	f 3 10
f 9 10	199	" Glass Mountain "	f 2 40
f 9 35	210	" Scarface..... "	f 2 20
f10 00	222	" Lookout..... "	f 1 55
10 30	234	Ar Bieber........Lv	1 30
		Western Pacific	
11 30	234	Lv Bieber........Ar	12 30
9 00	350	" Keddie....... "	3 30
2 15	426	" Oroville...... "	11 00
5 10	492	" Sacramento... "	7 00
7 45	537	" Stockton..... "	3 40
2 00	624	" Oakland...... "	10 00
	631	Ar San Francisco Lv	....
		See Note.	

Note—The line of the Great Northern between Klamath Falls, Ore., and Bieber, Cal., and the connecting line of the Western Pacific Bieber to Keddie, Cal., where it joins its main line into San Francisco, is used only for the handling of freight, except that mixed train service is operated on irregular schedule between Bend, Ore., and Bieber for the accommodation of local business. Persons intending to use this service should ascertain from the local Agent the time the train in either direction will depart from a station as the schedule is apt to vary each day. No through passenger train service is operated over this new line.

One of the first public timetables to cover the new BIEBER ROUTE through Central Oregon to California was this one issued in July, 1933. The map shows the route followed.

At the same time, the Western Pacific Railroad had constructed trackage northward from their main line in California to complete a connection with GN. The last spike was driven at Bieber, California on November 10, 1931. The GN Bieber route was a "come-lately" line and, although very profitable for freight moving, regular passenger service was never offered to the public.

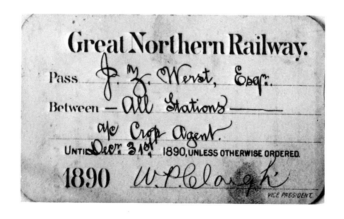

An artist's conception of a great man and his vision to build a railroad across the continent and on to California. Hill never lived to see the line built from the Pacific Northwest to California.

Butte Falls station taken during World War I

PACIFIC & EASTERN RAILWAY
COMPANY

Formerly known as the Medford & Crater Lake Railroad operating from Medford to Butte Falls, this short, thirty-four mile line was purchased by James J. Hill to use it as a part of an extension into the Rogue River Valley, and possibly later into California. The line remained many miles from any physical connection with the Hill tracks. At last, when Hill abandoned hope of entering California via this route, the line was sold.

| Read Down | | | | MEDFORD—BUTTE FALLS | | Read Up | |
3 Mon. Wed. Fri.	5 Mon. Wed. Fri.	1 Tue. Thur. Sat.	Miles	PACIFIC AND EASTERN RAILROAD	2 Tue. Thur. Sat.	6 Mon. Wed. Fri.	4 Mon. Wed. Fri.
. . . .	. . .	12 45	0.0	Lv . . . . Butte Falls . . . . Ar	11 15	. . . . . .	. . . . .
. . . .	. . . .	1 30	9.2	. . . . Derby	10 30	. . . . . .	. . . . .
. . . .	. . . .	2 05	16.8	. . . . School House Gap	9 55	. . . . . .	. . . . .
5 00	10 30	2 25	20.0	. . . . Eagle Point	9 45	9 45	4 55
5 12	10 42	2 40	23.2	. . . . Table Rock	9 29	9 29	4 40
5 17	10 47	2 45	24.7	. . . . Agate	9 24	9 24	4 35
5 40	11 15	3 15	31.7	Ar . . . . Medford Lv	9 00	9 00	4 15

CHAPTER 16

LEBANON (SP)

The Albany and Lebanon Railroad, an eleven-mile line running from Albany due east to the town of Lebanon, was built by the Oregon & California Railroad Company with little thought for its traffic potential, but mainly to discourage narrow gauge competitors from building into Lebanon.

Yet the Oregonian Railway Company, Ltd., had already announced plans for a narrow gauge track from Ray's Landing on the Willamette River that would cross the O&C at Woodburn and pass down the eastern edge of the Willamette Valley through Silverton, Lebanon, Scio and Brownsville. The ORR had driven their first spike at Silverton on April 19, 1880, a move that prevented Villard from building a Salem-to-Silverton line and which effectively bottled up Silverton.

But building trackage into Lebanon did not succeed in stopping the narrow gauge interests from constructing their railroad down the valley. The ORR merely built several miles to the west, through a station called Lebanon Junction which is now known as Tallman.

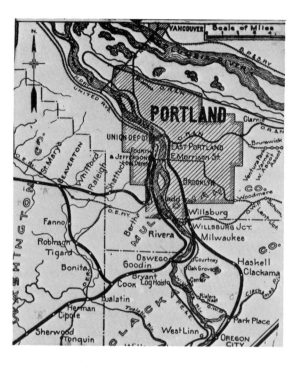

Upper left, Vale Kimes, the agent at Lebanon. *Upper right,* The BEAVERTON & WILLSBURG RAILROAD was built as a connection for lines "A", "B" and "C."

BEAVERTON & WILLSBURG RAILROAD COMPANY (SP)

This ten-mile railroad was built by Southern Pacific to connect three of their separate lines that all originated in Portland:

Line A, which began at Union Station, proceeded south on Fourth Street through Beaverton and Hillsboro. (The old Oregon Central Railroad Co.)

Line B, which originated at the Jefferson Street public wharf, proceeded south through Oswego and Newberg. (Originally the old narrow gauge Portland & Willamette Valley Railroad Co., a division of the Oregonian Railway Company, Ltd. By this time, however, the line had been converted to standard gauge.)

Line C, which began at Union Station, crossed the Willamette River to East Portland, and proceeded south through Clackamas, Oregon City and Salem. (The old Oregon & California East Side Division.)

Portland was a growing metropolis and its government's plans for the future did not include the operation of steam freight and passenger trains on downtown's Fourth Street. Responding to the problem, the SP constructed seven miles of track from Beaverton to Cook and three miles from Oswego to Willsburg Junction, which included a bridge across the Willamette. The new rail line, known as the Beaverton & Willsburg Railroad, permitted interchange among the three old lines and was especially valuable for freights leaving the Brooklyn freight yards.

WEST SIDE SUBDIVISION: Beaverton and Willsburg

			Second Class		First Class				TIME TABLE No. 61 July 17, 1910 STATIONS			First Class		Second Class		
	Eastward	**FROM SAN FRANCISCO**					DISTANCE FROM BEAVERTON			DISTANCE FROM PORTLAND				**TOWARD SAN FRANCISCO** Westward		
			56 Freight Daily Ex. Sun.		**8** Eureka & Monroe Passenger Daily	**4** Sheridan Passenger Daily						**7** Eureka & Monroe Passenger Daily	**3** Sheridan Passenger Daily		**55** Freight Daily Ex. Sun.	
			P M L 2.20		A M L 11.06	A M L 9.05	0.0	D R BEAVERTON	20.6		P M A 1.56	P M A 5.12		A M A 8.00	
			2.35		11.12	9.12	2.3	Fanno (Spur)	18.3		1.49	5.05		7.55	
			2.40		11.15	9.15	3.0	Scholls (Spur)	17.6		1.46	5.02		7.50	
			2.45		11.17	9.17	3.8	Oregon Electric Crossing (Siding)	16.8		1.44	5.00		7.45	
			2.50		11.19	9.19	4.6	Tigard	16.0		1.42	4.58		7.40	
			2.55		11.22	9.23	6.0	Bonita (Spur)	14.6		1.38	4.54		7.35	
			3.00 P M A		11.25 A M A	9.26 A M A	7.4	R COOK	13.2		1.35 P M L	4.51 P M L		7.30 A M L	
			P M L 3.30			A M L 9.38	11.3	D R OSWEGO	9.3			P M A 4.40		A M A 7.10	
			3.45			9.45	13.6	Milwaukee	7.0			4.29		6.56	
			3.50 P M L			9.52 A M A	14.7	WILLSBURG JCT.	5.9			4.25 P M L		6.52 A M L	
			Daily Ex. Sun.		Daily	Daily					Daily	Daily		Daily Ex. Sun.	
			1.00		0.19	0.35		Time Over District	10.8		0.21	0.36		0.18	
			10.8		39.37	18.34		Average Speed per Hour			21.14	18.00		13.05	

West bound trains are superior to trains of same class in opposite direction. (See Rule 72).

Main track switches at Oswego and Cook, when not in use, will be left set and locked for Yamhill main track.

For schedule of trains between Cook and Oswego see pages 10 and 11.

CHAPTER 17

COOS BAY, ROSEBURG &
EASTERN RAILROAD AND
NAVIGATION COMPANY (SP)

This twenty-six mile railroad, popularly called the Coos Bay & Eastern, was built from Myrtle Point to Marshfield (Coos Bay) in 1893. The road hauled a great deal of freight, logs and local passengers, in addition to coal, a major commodity supplied by the Beaver Hill mine. A large bunker was constructed in the yards at Marshfield on the bay in front of the present station. Coal was dumped here later to be loaded into colliers for ocean shipment.

For many years the line was isolated from outside rail connections. Eventually Southern Pacific added steamer service from Portland to Marshfield several times a week. In 1916 the SP completed trackage that connected the CBR&E&N with their main line at Eugene.

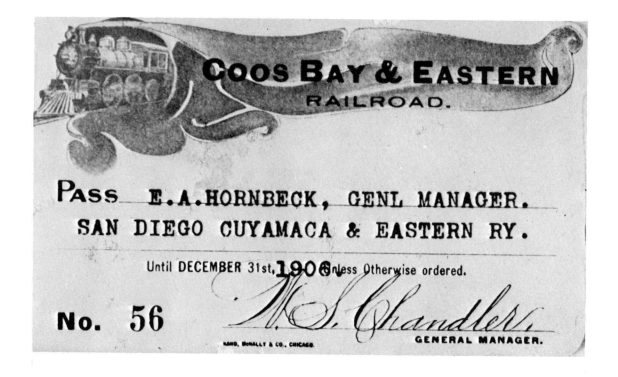

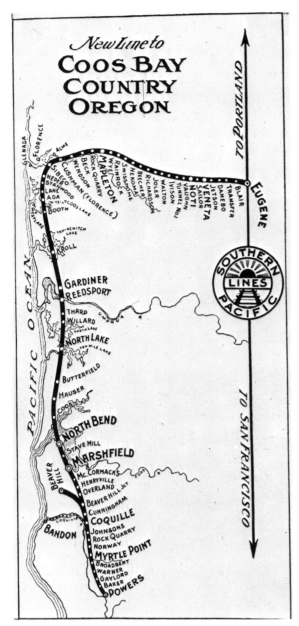

New Line to
COOS BAY
COUNTRY
OREGON

SHASTA ROUTE
CONNECTING LINES

PORTLAND & COOS BAY STEAMSHIP LINE
OPERATES THE
Fine Steamer Breakwater
BETWEEN
PORTLAND & COOS BAY POINTS
Connecting at Marshfield, Oregon with Coos Bay, Roseburg & Eastern
Railroad and Navigation Company
LEAVES PORTLAND WEDNESDAYS, 8 p. m., FROM AINSWORTH DOCK
*Freight will be received till 4:00 p. m.
on day of departure.*

LEAVES COOS BAY SATURDAYS
AT SERVICE OF TIDE

PASSENGER RATES BETWEEN PORTLAND AND COOS BAY
First Cabin, - - $10.00   Second Cabin, - - 7.00
INCLUDING BERTH AND MEALS.
Ticket Offices: Third and Washington Streets, Portland
OR AINSWORTH DOCK
ALSO MARSHFIELD, COOS BAY.

COOS BAY, ROSEBURG & EASTERN RAILROAD

No. 3 Ex. Sun	No. 1 Ex. Sun	STATIONS	No. 2 Ex. Sun	No. 4 Ex. Sun	
1.00	8.00	Lv.. MARSHFIELD ..Ar	12.00	4.30	
1.35	f8.35	....Summit	f11.00	3.55	
1.45	8.45	Ar... Junction Lv	10.50	3.45	
1.50		..Ar.... Beaver Hill ...Lv		2.45	
	9.10	Lv.... Coquille ....Ar	10.27		
	f9.20	Lv.... Johnsons	f10.20		
	f9.25	....Schroeders	f10.10		
	f9.30	....Norway	f10.05		
	9.40	Ar..MYRTLE POINT..Lv	10.00		

A Shasta Route Timetable, 1912

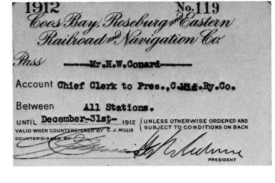

1912   No.119
Coos Bay, Roseburg and Eastern
Railroad and Navigation Co.

Pass ------Mr. H. W. Conard------

Account Chief Clerk to Pres., C. B. R. & E. Ry. Co.

Between   All Stations.

UNTIL December-31st- 1912 { UNLESS OTHERWISE ORDERED AND
VALID WHEN COUNTERSIGNED BY C. J. MILLIS { SUBJECT TO CONDITIONS ON BACK
COUNTERSIGNED BY

PRESIDENT

NEW TRAIN

=BETWEEN=

Eugene and Marshfield

COMMENCING SATURDAY, JUNE 15

An additional train daily (No. 501 and 502) between Eugene and Marshfield. No change in No. 503 and 504.

Read Down				Read Up	
No. 504	No. 502			No. 501	No. 503
1:10am	1:00pm	Lv Eugene Ar		s12:01pm	s 1:10am
1:36	1:28	Maywood		11:29am	12:28
1:43	1:35	Veneta		s11:22	s12:18
1:48	1:41	Elrus		11:16	12:10
1:56	1:45	Noti		11:12	12:05am
2:03	1.52	Vaughan		11:03	11:54pm
2:10	2.01	Flagg		10:55	11:43
2:22	2:13	Walton		10:43	11:30
2:38	2:29	Austa		10:30	11:14
2:48	2:38	Richardson		10:22	11:05
2:54	2:47	Beecher		10:13	10:56
3:08	3.04	Nekoma		9:56	10:44
3:18	3:13	Swisshome		9:46	10:37
3:26	3:22	Rainrock		9:36	10:29
s 3:40	s 3:35	Mapleton		s 9:23	s10:20
3:54	3:50	Beck		9:04	10:05
4:00	3:56	Betzen		8:58	10:00
4:07	4:04	Wendson		8:51	9:53
s 4:15	s 4:08	Cushman		s 8:48	s 9:50
4:21	4:13	Siboco		8:45	9:39
4:30	4:21	Canary		8:34	9:32
s 4:43	s 4:29	Siltcoos		s 8:24	s 9:25
4:50	4:35	Ada		8:18	9:19
4:54	4:38	Booth		8:16	9:16
5:09	4:50	Kroll		8:05	9:06
5:15	4:57	Brenham		7:59	9:01
s 5:30	s 5:06	Gardiner		s 7:49	s 8:53
s 5:40	s 5:20	Reedsport		s 7:40	s 8:45
6:00	5:29	Tharp		7:28	8:28
s 6:20	s 5:43	Lakeside		s 7:13	s 8:13
6:40	5:56	Hauser		6:58	7:59
6:50	6:05	Coos		6:50	7:52
s 7:05	s 6:20	North Bend		s 6:35	s 7:43
s 7:25am	s 6:35pm	Marshfield (Cen. Ave.) Lv		s 6:25am	s 7:30pm

s Regular Stops --- at other stations, stops on flag. Connections at Eugene to and from North and South

Low Round Trip Fares to Portland

Marshfield to Portland, and return $13.75   Reedsport to Portland, and return $11.95

North Bend to Portland, and return 13.55   Mapleton to Portland, and return 9.70

Similar Fares From Other Stations

Planning a trip? Call on our local agent for travel information

Southern Pacific

A-62 6-15-29 1250

Coquille, 1910

Myrtle Point, 1910

Here's a picture of the first train to make this coast run from Eugene on August 24, 1916. Dozens of eager spectators greeted the old funnel-stacked engine and train at every station and stop along the scenic route, North Bend, Oregon.

Reedsport during World War I

This line was constructed from Eugene to Mapleton (58 miles) under the name of the Willamette
Pacific Railroad. It eventually became a part of the SP's Coos Bay line.

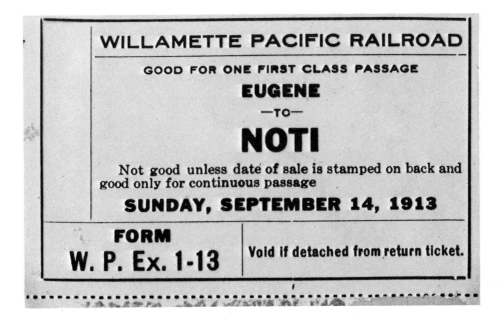

CHAPTER 18

CALIFORNIA & NORTHEASTERN RAILROAD—The Cascade Line (SP)

A private company had built northward from the Southern Pacific's main line at Weed toward Klamath Falls. Before the California & Northeastern Railroad reached Klamath Falls, however, the SP had purchased it. They continued the construction program, carrying the Cascade Line on to Oakridge and into Eugene.

With its completion, a new main line, which divided at Eugene and came together again at Black Butte, California, was opened. It was twenty-three miles shorter than the old Siskiyou main line (via Roseburg and Ashland) and had lighter grade and less curvature.

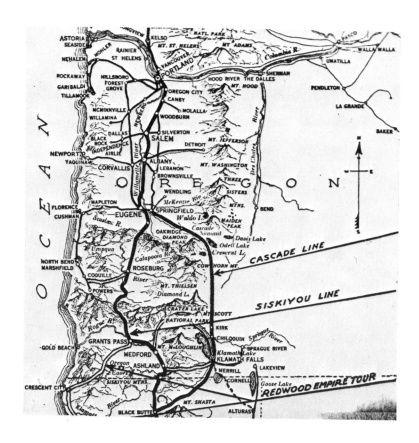

CALIFORNIA & OREGON COAST RAILROAD CO.

CALIFORNIA AND OREGON COAST RAILROAD

ROBERT E. TWOHY, President,
JAMES F. TWOHY, Vice-President,
R. B. MILLER, Vice-President,
JOHN HAMPSHIRE, Secretary-Treasurer,
PRESTON DELANO, General Manager,
GEO. W. BOSCHKE, Chief Engineer,

Grants Pass, Ore.

Trains marked † run daily, except Sunday.

STANDARD—*Pacific time.*

Connection.—At Grants Pass—With Southern Pacific Co.

No. 1	Mls	*December 1, 1916.*	No. 2	
†10 00 A M	0	lve...**Grants Pass**..arr.	2 00 P M	
10 05 ,,	2	......Allen Creek......	1 47 ,,	
10 12 ,,	4	......Band Creek......	1 45 ,,	
10 16 ,,	5	......Simmons........	1 39 ,,	
10 24 ,,	7	...Jerome Prairie...	1 31 ,,	
10 28 ,,	8	......Arden Craig.....	1 27 ,,	
10 40 ,,	10	......Wilderville......	1 20 ,,	
10 44 ,,	11	......Prairie Creek....	1 11 ,,	
10 50 ,,	13	........Wonder.......	1 06 ,,	
11 00 A M	15	arr.**Waters Creek**.lve.	†1 00 P M	

Klamath Falls in 1924

This is not a station in the south seas, but a railroad resting point on the Cascade Line between Eugene and Klamath Falls.

Ride 'um cowboy! A Sunday afternoon celebration. Oakridge was the end of the line from the Woodburn-Brownsville-Natron line for many years. On September 1, 1926, a connection was opened to Klamath Falls.

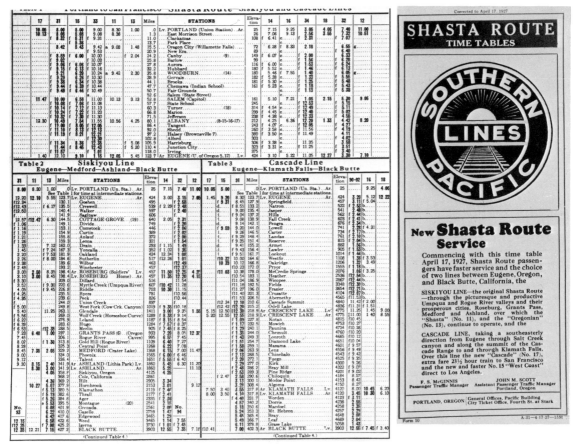

Upper left, A timetable for the Shasta Route. *Below,* Westfir was one of the many railroad stations in service to handle a logging community's needs. Forestry and forest products are Oregon's billion dollar industry.

Lakeview station

NEVADA-CALIFORNIA-OREGON
RAILWAY (SP)

A narrow gauge line, the Nevada-California-Oregon Railway originated at Reno, Nevada and was to terminate at The Dalles, Oregon. It reached Lakeview in January of 1912 and was never built beyond this point. The Southern Pacific purchased the line and converted it to standard gauge.

This photograph shows the arrival of the first standard gauge train at Lakeview station, September 1, 1928.

The CALIFORNIA & OREGON COAST RAILROAD's "Yellow Streak" in front of the railroad station. A slight lack of confidence in the vehicle caused it to be known as the "Yellow Peril." The line operated from Grants Pass to Waters Creek, a fifteen mile trip.

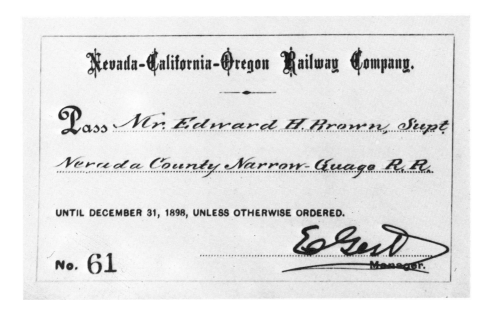

Nevada-California-Oregon Railway Company.

Pass Mr. Edward H. Brown, Supt.

Nevada County Narrow Guage R.R.

UNTIL DECEMBER 31, 1898, UNLESS OTHERWISE ORDERED.

No. 61

Manager.

CHAPTER 19

CORVALLIS & ALSEA RIVER
RAILWAY COMPANY (SP)

Built by Stephen Carver in 1908, this line extended for some thirty miles from Corvallis south to Monroe, Alpine and Glenbrook. The line was intended originally to be constructed on to Alsea and thence to the Pacific Coast, but the panic of 1909 prevented Carver from securing adequate credit to finance the remainder of the road.

In 1911, Alvadore Welch purchased the C&AR along with the streetcar systems of Salem, Albany, West Linn and Eugene with the idea that these lines would be the nucleus for an electric railroad to be built from Portland to San Francisco. But in 1912 the Portland Eugene & Eastern Railway Company (Welch's corporation) was sold to the Southern Pacific.

The Chief Engineer of the Corvallis & Alsea Railroad Company traveling over the line in his automobile equipped with flange wheels.

This photograph shows the "Goose" in front of the makeshift station at Carver

PORTLAND & OREGON CITY
RAILWAY COMPANY

The Portland & Oregon City Railway was a small, fifteen-mile independent line constructed in 1913-14 from East Portland, near the SP tracks at Hawthorne Avenue, to the Clackamas River. Later it was extended to Baker Bridge in Clackamas County. Its terminus was named Carver, in honor of the railroad builder. "The Goose." a quaint gasoline-powered car, chugged from Carver to Portland several times a day.

CHAPTER 20

OREGON & SOUTHEASTERN
RAILROAD COMPANY

The Oregon & Southeastern Railroad was built from Cottage Grove to Disston during the period from 1902 through 1906 in order to reach and serve the Bohemia gold mines located thirty-five miles southeast of Cottage Grove and eighty miles from the coast in the Calapooya Mountains. After the gold mines petered out, forest products kept the railroad operating.

Culp's Creek is one of the stations along the twenty mile right-of-way. Today it is one of the largest plywood mills in the state. The town was originally homesteaded by John Culp, who realized the tremendous potential of lumbering in the area.

In 1912 the line was reorganized and its name changed to the Oregon Pacific & Eastern Railway.

This photo shows No. 3 spot pulling a carload of Oregon logs into Cottage Grove for the mill. The railroad station can be seen in the background.

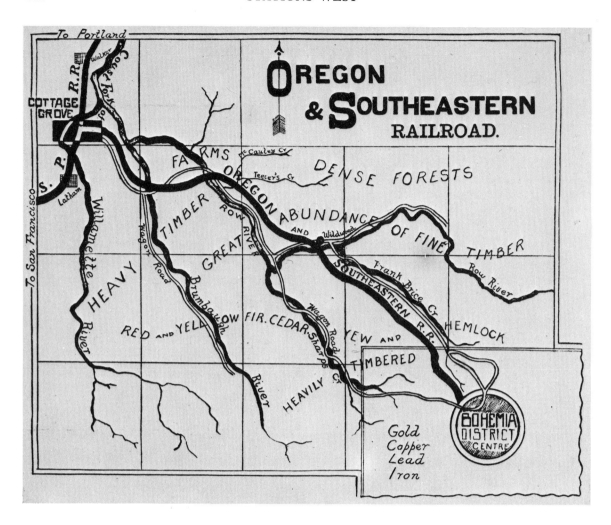

	Tues. and Sat.	Daily Ex Sun	Miles	STATIONS	Daily Ex Sun	Tues. and Sun.	
....	2.30	7.30	0	Lv....COTTAGE GROVE....Ar	12.00	5.15	....
....	3.00	8.14	8	................Dorena...............	11.08	4.44	....
....	3.38	9.15	16	..............Wildwood..............	10.15	4.17	....
....	3.50	9.45	......	Ar............Disston............Lv	10.00	4.00	....

OREGON AND SOUTHEASTERN RAILROAD

An OREGON PACIFIC & EASTERN train prepares to leave Village Green for a trip over the line

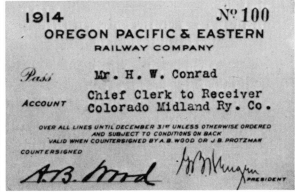

WILLAMINA & GRAND RONDE RAILWAY COMPANY changed hands, the new company renaming it LONGVIEW, PORTLAND & NORTHERN RAILWAY CO. Shown above is one of the early steam engines now replaced by diesel.

WILLAMINA & GRAND RONDE RAILWAY COMPANY

This small line has only nine miles of track and connects with the Southern Pacific at Willamina. It is a public carrier handling forest products almost exclusively. In 1926, when Hollywood filmed *The General* starring Buster Keaton, it was a W&GR engine that the actor piloted.

Mrs. Alida Wegner was agent at Grand Ronde for many years.

"The Texas," near Cottage Grove in 1926. "The General" can be seen in the distance

In 1926, Buster Keaton and company filmed *The General* along the OREGON & SOUTHEASTERN RAILWAY COMPANY tracks. The scene originally transpired in Georgia in 1862. The story is somewhat altered from the true account, but it did make a thrilling movie. The two locomotives, "The Texas" and "The General," are in hot pursuit as the story goes. Buster Keaton, the hero, on "The General," the lead engine, sets fire to the bridge and "The Texas," attempting to follow, drops into the drink, as shown in the photograph. During the filming, Cottage Grove and the OSE were very active. The regular daily OSE train operated early in the morning in order to give the film company complete freedom in making the movie.

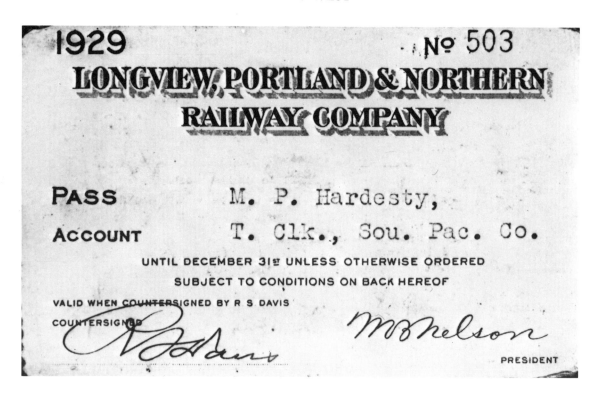

This line had only two and one-half miles of track from Monmouth to Independence. They operated, under contract, sixteen miles for the Southern Pacific, from Dallas to Airlie. This photo shows the arrival of the I&M-1243 at Monmouth. This city is the home of the state teachers college.

The I&M speeder picks up a few passengers at Airlie. This town is the end of the old Oregonian Railway Co., Ltd. The narrow gauge tracks of this line later became a part of the Southern Pacific lines.

INDEPENDENCE, MONMOUTH, AIRLIE
Independence & Monmouth Ry.

No. 70 Daily	No. 73 Motor Daily	No. 66 Daily	No. 68 Daily	No. 61 Daily	No. 64 Daily	STATIONS	No. 62 Daily	No. 65 Daily	No. 69 Daily	No. 73 Daily	No. 72 Daily	No. 71 Daily
6.15	3.10	2.05	10.05	6.35	6.15	Lv..INDEPENDENCE..Ar	8.15	9.15	1.40	.....	5.45	8.05
6.30	.....	2.15	11.20	.....	6.35	..Monmouth...	8.05	8.55	1.25	3.45	.....	7.45
6.39	.....	2.24	11.29	.....	6.44	...Cochrane...	.....	8.46	1.16	3 36	.....	7.34
6.55	.....	3.46	11.45	.....	7.00	Ar..DALLAS..Lv	.....	8.30	1.00	3.20	.....	7.20
.....	3.45	.....	.....	6.40	.....	Lv..Monmouth...Ar	8.00	.....	.....	.....	5.35	.....
.....	4.00	.....	.....	6.55	.....	...Elkins...	7.45	.....	.....	.....	5.20	.....
.....	4.10	.....	.....	7.05	.....	...Simpson...	7.35	.....	.....	.....	5.10	.....
.....	4.20	.....	.....	7.15	.....	Ar..AIRLIE..Lv	7.25	.....	.....	.....	5.00	.....

1913   No. 0059
INDEPENDENCE & MONMOUTH
RAILWAY COMPANY

PASS Mr. H. W. Conard,

ACCOUNT Chief Clerk to President,

The Colorado Midland Ry. Co.

BETWEEN All Stations.

UNTIL DECEMBER 31, 1912

UNLESS OTHERWISE ORDERED AND SUBJECT TO CONDITIONS ON BACK

VALID WHEN COUNTERSIGNED BY

H. HIRSCHBERG   *H. Hirschberg.*

PRESIDENT

This photograph of Independence was taken in 1913. John Bewley, Engineer, and Walter L. Smith, Conductor, are pictured.

This photo of the KLAMATH FALLS MUNICIPAL RAILWAY No. 1 was taken before the line became a part of the OC&E.

Sidings	Other Tracks	SECOND CLASS 2 Freight Daily Ex. Sunday	Distance from Klamath Falls	TIME TABLE No. 2 Effective February 16, 1941 — STATIONS	Telegraph Calls	Distance from Bly	SIGNS	SECOND CLASS 1 Freight Daily Ex. Sunday
Yard	366	L 11.30 AM		KLAMATH FALLS		63.39	PXY	A 9.55 PM
				3.59				
11	13	11.40	3.59	HAGER		59.80	P	9.40
				1.64				
	10	11.46	5.23	PINE GROVE		58.16		9.30
				2.27				
	5	11.53	7.50	OLENE		55.89	P	9.22
				4.80				
	48	12.08 PM	12.30	SWAN LAKE		51.09		9.07
				2.83				
31		12.18	15.13	MOYINA		48.81	PW	8.55
				2.22				
	38	12.25	17.35	DAIRY		46.04	PY	8.45
				4.00				
	55	12.37	21.35	HILDEBRAND		42.04	P	8.30
				3.78				
21		12.49	25.13	HORTON		38.26	PX	8.15
				6.60				
	32	1.10	31.73	WEST SWITCH BACK		31.66	P	7.50
				1.23				
	32	1.20	32.96	EAST SWITCH BACK		30.43		7.35
				4.82				
62	100	1.50	37.78	SPRAGUE RIVER	SR	25.61	DPWXY	7.05
				12.97				
32	26	2.30	50.75	BEATTY		12.64	PX	6.15
				0.48				
		2.32	51.23	SYCAN		12.16	P	6.13
				0.58				
		2.34	51.81	KESTERSON SPUR		11.58		6.11
				7.65				
	25	3.00	59.46	NORTH FORK		3.93		5.40
				3.93				
Yard	122	A 3.15 PM	63.39	BLY	BY		DPRWXY	L 5.15 PM
		3.45 / 16.9		Time over Subdivision / Average Speed Per Hour				4.40 / 13.5

EASTWARD TRAINS ARE SUPERIOR TO WESTWARD TRAINS OF THE SAME CLASS.

An OREGON, CALIFORNIA & EASTERN RAILWAY timetable issued February 16, 1941

OREGON, CALIFORNIA & EASTERN RAILWAY (BN–SP)

Often referred to as the Strahorn Line for its promoter Robert E. Strahorn, the original plan for this railway was to run from Klamath Falls on the Southern Pacific, to Bend on the Oregon Trunk, to Crane on the Union Pacific, and at last to Lakeview on the Nevada-California-Oregon Railway. With these connections, the OC&E would be able to serve much of the southeastern portion of the state. Strahorn's ultimate object was to interest one of the major railroads to whom he would connect in the eventual purchase of his line.

In 1919 Strahorn secured the Klamath Falls Municipal Railway, which operated the twenty miles from Klamath Falls to Dairy. This railway became the first portion of the OC&E. By 1929, the line had reached the small settlement of Bly, sixty-three miles from Klamath Falls, and was never built beyond it. The Southern Pacific acquired the line shortly thereafter and sold Great Northern half-interest in it. Today the railroad handles mostly forest products.

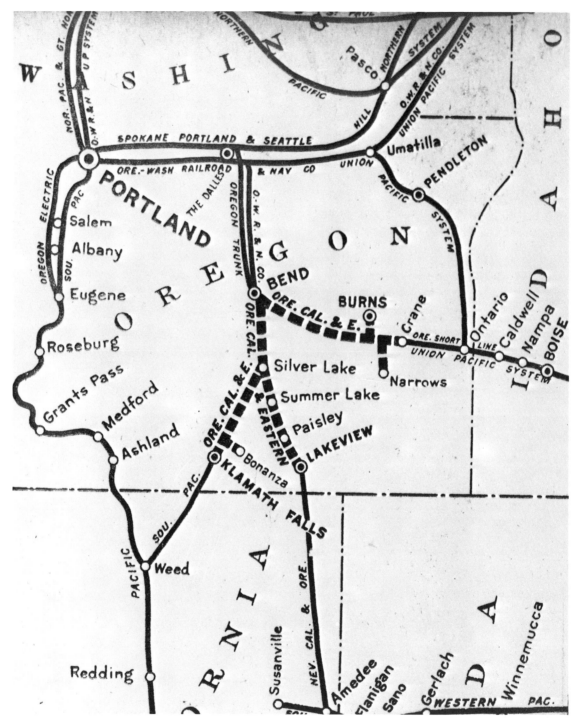

This map of the OREGON, CALIFORNIA & EASTERN RAILWAY shows the proposed connections with public carriers at Klamath Falls, Bend, Crane and Lakeview. The line was actually only built sixty-three miles, to Bly.

CHAPTER 21

SALEM, FALLS CITY & WESTERN
RAILWAY COMPANY (SP)

Louis Gerlinger and Charles K. Spaulding purchased 7,000 acres of timberland in the Black Rock area of central Polk County. To market their large stands of timber, they built the SFC&W as a logging railroad. In 1903, Gerlinger built his rail line from Dallas to Falls City, a distance of ten miles, and a year later he extended his line another three miles to Black Rock.

He also built a large sawmill at Dallas, knowing that this small town would offer

his mill workers the community life that a backwoods boomtown could not. Also by building in Dallas, he had access to the Airlie Branch of the Southern Pacific tracks. These two factors would allow for future mill expansion. His farsightedness was to result in the Willamette Valley Lumber Company, now known as Willamette Industries, one of the largest producers of forest products in the Pacific Northwest.

Gerlinger once said: "I know some-

On September 13, 1909, the first train pulled into West Salem with Fritz, one of the Gerlinger boys, at the throttle of the locomotive. Ferry service was used to cross the river into Salem. In 1913, a railroad bridge was constructed across the Willamette River allowing through train service into Salem.

McKeen car crossing the Willamette River at Salem on SFC&W, about 1914

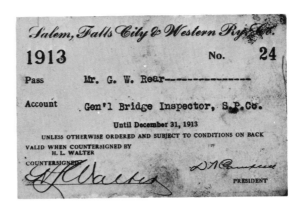

SALEM-FALLS CITY AND WESTERN RAILWAY

——OPERATING DAILY TRAINS——

Between Salem, Dallas, Falls City, Black Rock

L. GERLINGER, PRESIDENT.

General Office Gerlinger Bldg.

Second and Alder Streets,   PORTLAND, OR.

thing about the lumber business but darn little about railroad management." He must have been pleased, therefore, when the Southern Pacific took over the operation of the SFC&W. Under the SP's ownership the SFC&W continued building from Dallas through Eola and West Salem, and on to a connection with their own line in Salem.

Salem, Falls City & Western Ry. Co.

1913   No.   24

Pass   Mr. G. W. Rear————————

Account   Gen'l Bridge Inspector, S.P.Co.

Until December 31, 1913

UNLESS OTHERWISE ORDERED AND SUBJECT TO CONDITIONS ON BACK

VALID WHEN COUNTERSIGNED BY
H. L. WALTER

COUNTERSIGNED

PRESIDENT

Falls City, 1905

ISSUED BY

SALEM, FALLS CITY & WESTERN RY. CO.

Non-Transferable Saturday to Monday Excursion Ticket

GOOD SUBJECT TO THE CONDITIONS PRINTED BELOW FOR

ONE CONTINUOUS FIRST CLASS PASSAGE

TO

PORTLAND, ORE.

AND RETURN.

Via Route designated in coupons attached. when officially stamped and sold by the Company's Agent.

SUBJECT TO THE FOLLOWING CONTRACT AND CONDITIONS:

1st. **Going Trip.** Must be used for continuous passage to destination on the Saturday or Sunday of date stamped on back.

2nd. **Return Trip.** Must be completed on or before first Monday following sale date.

3rd. **Stop-overs.** Will not be allowed on either going or return trip.

4th. **Non-transferable.** The ticket is not transferable.

5th. **Baggage** liability is limited to wearing apparel not to exceed One Hundred Dollars in value for a whole ticket and Fifty Dollars for a half ticket.

6th. **Alterations.** This ticket is void if coupons are detached from contract or if any alterations or erasures are made hereon.

7th. **Responsibility.** In selling this ticket for passage over other lines and in checking baggage on it, the Salem, Fall City & Western Ry. Co. acts only as Agent and is not responsible beyond its own lines.

_____
Gen'l Pass. Agt

Via SALEM, FALLS CITY & WESTERN RY. CO.

GERLINGER TO DALLAS

On Conditions named in Contract and worthless if detached.

| Destination, PORTLAND AND RETURN | IF FOR HALF 1/2 |
| Form SM \| Sat.-Mon. Excursion | PUNCH HERE |

ISSUED BY
Salem, Falls City & Western Ry. Co.

SFC&W. SP-PS—SP-PS, SFC&W.

Via SOUTHERN PACIFIC CO. (Lines in Oregon)

PORTLAND TO GERLINGER

On Conditions named in Contract and worthless if detached.

| Destination, PORTLAND AND RETURN | IF FOR HALF 1/2 |
| Form SM \| Sat.-Mon. Excursion | PUNCH HERE |

ISSUED BY
Salem, Falls City & Western Ry. Co.

SFC&W. SP-PS—SP-PS, SFC&W.

LOCAL TIME TABLE
Salem, Falls City & Western Railway

WEST BOUND — 1911

STATIONS	Miles from W. Salem	PASSENGER Daily Except Sunday			PASSENGER Sunday Only		
		No. 2 A.M.	No. 4 P.M.	No. 6 P.M.	No. 10 A.M.	No. 12 P.M.	No 14 P.M.
West Salem Lv.	0	9 00	1 30	4 35	9 00	1 35	5 50
†Kingwood Park	0	9 03	1 33	4 38	9 03	1 38	5 53
†Log Dump	2	9 06	1 36	4 41	9 06	1 41	5 56
†Eola	4	9 10	1 40	4 45	9 10	1 45	6 00
†McNary	6	9 14	1 44	4 49	9 14	1 49	6 04
†Greenwood	7	9 18	1 48	4 53	9 18	1 53	6 08
†Derry Orchard	8	9 21	1 51	4 56	9 21	1 56	6 11
So. Pac. Cross'g	9	9 22	1 52	4 57	9 22	1 57	6 12
†Rickreal!	10	9 24	1 54	4 59	9 24	1 59	6 14
†Bowersville	11	9 27	1 57	5 02	9 27	2 02	6 17
DALLAS Ar.	14	9 40	2 10	5 15	9 40	2 15	6 30
DALLAS Lv.	14	9 45	2 15	5 20	9 45	2 20	
†Teats	18	10 00	2 30	5 35	10 00	2 35	
†Gilliam	19	10 02	2 32	5 37	10 02	2 37	
†Bridgeport	21	10 06	2 36	5 41	10 06	2 41	
Falls City	24	10 15	2 45	5 50	10 15	2 50	
Black Rock	27	10 35			10 35	3 10	

EAST BOUND

STATIONS	Miles from B. Rock	PASSENGER Daily Except Sunday				PASSENGER Sunday Only		
		No. 3 A.M.	No. 5 A.M.	No. 7 P.M.	No. 9 P.M.	No. 11 A.M.	No. 13 A.M.	No. 15 P.M.
Black Rock Lv.	0		11 00				11 45	4 00
Falls City	3		11 15	3 00	6 05		12 00	4 15
†Bridgeport	6		11 24	3 09	6 14		12 09	4 24
†Gilliam	8		11 28	3 13	6 18		12 13	4 28
†Teats	9		11 30	3 15	6 20		12 15	4 30
DALLAS Ar	13		11 45	3 30	6 35		12 30	4 45
DALLAS Lv.	13	7 35	11 50	3 35		7 35	12 35	4 50
†Bowersville	16	7 48	12 03	3 48		7 48	12 48	5 03
†Rickreall	17	7 51	12 06	3 51		7 51	12 51	5 06
So. Pac. Cross'g	18	7 52	12 07	3 52		7 52	12 52	5 07
†Derry Orchard	19	7 54	12 09	3 54		7 54	12 54	5 09
†Greenwood	20	7 57	12 12	3 57		7 57	12 57	5 12
†McNary	21	8 01	12 16	4 01		8 01	1 01	5 16
†Eola	23	8 05	12 20	4 05		8 05	1 05	5 20
†Log Dump	25	8 09	12 24	4 09		8 09	1 09	5 24
†Kingwood Park	8	8 12	12 27	4 12		8 12	1 12	5 27
West Salem	27	8 15	12 30	4 15		8 15	1 15	5 30

†Trains Stop on Signal Only.

Stanley Olson was the agent at Gerlinger Station for many years.

Jacksonville

RRV No. 2 at the station in Medford

SOUTHERN OREGON TRACTION COMPANY No. 1 in Medford about 1915. This car performed service between Medford and Jacksonville.

ROGUE RIVER VALLEY RAILROAD

4 Daily	2 Daily	Miles	STATIONS	1 Daily	3 Daily	
....	5 35	10.40	0	Lv. ....MEDFORD ....Ar	9.20	3 50	....
....	6.15	11.00	6	Ar......... Jacksonville Lv	9.00	3 30	....

Trains stop at Thomas, Harbaugh and Davisville on signal only.

MOTOR CAR SERVICE

Leaves Medford daily, 8.00 a. m., 9 00 p. m. and 12 50 p. m.
Leaves Jacksonville daily, 7.00 a. m., 11.30 a. m. and 7.30 p. m.

YREKA RAILROAD

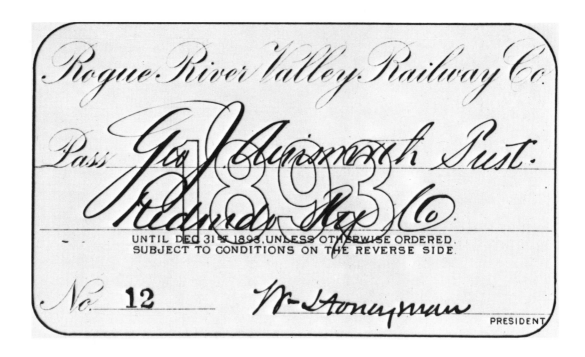

The V&S was a public carrier railroad handling mostly forest products. The line was recently purchased by the Boise Cascade Corporation.

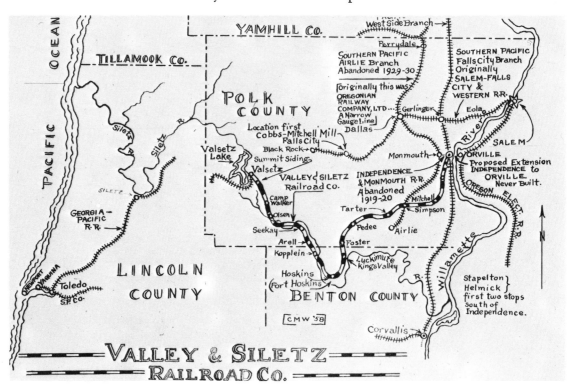

Above, Jack Barton, the agent at Independence.   *Below,* V&S Motor No. 5 stops in front of the Independence station. Note the lack of paint on the station and on the box car. This photograph was taken in 1945.

Valley & Siletz Railroad Company

| Eastward | | | | | | HOSKINS DIVISION | | | | Westward | | |

Second Class		First Class			Miles from Independence	TIME TABLE NO. 1 Effective January 1st, 1918. STATIONS	Capacity of Tracks in Cars	First Class			Second Class	
24 Mixed	22 Mixed										21 Mixed	23 Mixed
Daily except Sunday	Daily except Sunday										Daily except Sunday	Daily except Sunday
P.M. 2.40	A.M.				0	....Independence.R 1-8	PWF 22				A.M.	P.M. 3.00
f 2.34					1.8	....Stapleton...... 1-8	6					f 3.07
f 2.27					3.6	....Neahr........ 1-7						f 3.14
f 2.20					5.3	....Helmick...... 2-2						f 3.21
f 2.12					7.5	....Mitchell...... 09	7					f 3.30
					8.4	...S. P. Crossing.. 0-4						
f 2.05					8.8	....Simpson...... 1-3	P					f 3.36
2.00	7.50				10.1	....Crisp ....R 0-7	22				8.15	3.50
f 1.38	f 7.45				10.8	....Tartar 1-9	9				f 8.18	f 3.53
f 1.32	f 7.37				12.7	....Wallinch..... 2-1	P				f 8.27	f 4.03
1.20	7.30				14.8	....Pedee........ 2-5	6				8.35	4.12
f 1.08	f 7.20				17.3	....Ritner 1-5	24 P				f 8.50	f 4.28
12.55	7.13				18.8	Kings Valley.... 2-6	18				9.03	4.47
f 12.43 12.40	f 7.03				21.4	Tiff. 0-8					f 9.12	f 4.57
11.48	7.00				22.2	Hoskins ....R 3-6	PWF 43				9.35	5.00
f 11.35					25.8	....Kopplein 1-0					f 9.47	
f 11.30					26.8	....Arell 1-9	22 W				f 9.52	
f 11.20					28.7	Seekay 5-0					f 10.05	
10.55 A.M.	A.M.				33.7	Valsetz. R	P 22				10.30 A.M.	P.M.
2.53 11.69	.50 14.53					Time over District. Average Speed per Hour					2.15 10.49	2.00 11.10

Westward trains are superior to trains of same class in opposite direction (See Rule 72). Exceptions:
Train No. 22 is superior to Train No. 21, Train No. 24 is superior to Train No. 23.

V&S Timetable No. 1 issued January 1, 1918

Hoskins (Fort Hoskins) was established in 1856 and garrisoned with soldiers to protect the settlers from Indians.

A more modern view of Hoskins

1931   No. 7

VALLEY AND SILETZ RAILROAD COMPANY

Pass
Account   J. B. Clarke
Between   Auditor
                 All Stations

UNTIL DECEMBER 31, 1931, UNLESS OTHERWISE ORDERED
AND SUBJECT TO CONDITIONS ON BACK

VALID WHEN COUNTERSIGNED BY C. N. HUGGINS

Countersigned by

                                              PRESIDENT

V&S annual pass issued in 1931

V&S train at Valsetz ready to start the thirty-three mile trip to Independence. Half of the station
is used as a U.S. postoffice. This photograph was taken in 1958.

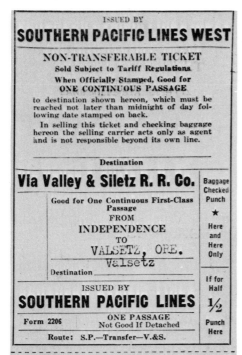

Dick Griffitts, the agent at Valsetz

CHAPTER 23

THE WILLAMETTE BRIDGE
RAILWAY COMPANY

The Willamette Bridge Railway Company was often referred to as a hybrid system, a cross between a street railway and a short line railroad. Its seven miles of trackage originated at a station located only a short distance from the east approach to the Steel Bridge or, as some called it, the Railroad Bridge in Portland.

The WBR's one or two coaches were pulled by Number 5, a regular locomotive (Brooks 4-4-0) formerly used on the Kansas Central. From the Stanton Street station the line cut a swath through the timber to its destination at St. Johns, stopping at such little towns as North Albina, Ockley Green, Arbor Lodge, Peninsula, University Park and Portsmouth, all of which are now a part of Portland.

From the West Side a streetcar, starting from Third and Morrison Streets and running over the Steel Bridge, made a connection with the WBR. In 1891 the line was absorbed by the City and Suburban Railway Company and eventually became a part of the streetcar system of Portland.

WILLAMETTE BRIDGE RAILWAY CO.
ST. JOHNS MOTOR LINE.

A M
6:15
8:50
10:15
11;10

AUG. 3

TRANSFER SLIP.

From St. Johns Motor Line to Electric Car Going West.

P M
1:25

This slip will not be honored unless presented at junction of Elliott and Hawley Sts., Albina Line, and is good only on this date and for trip indicated by punched mark in margin.

2:25
3:25
4:50

This photo shows Old Number 5 pulling a train through the station at Portsmouth. (Oregon Historical Society photo)

THE PORTLAND AND VANCOUVER RAILWAY

The P&V ran from the foot of East Stark Street in East Portland to Hayden Landing on the south bank of the Columbia River. A quarter would take a traveler for two ferry rides and a train trip—one of the best travel bargains of the day. Purchasing a ticket at the foot of Stark Street, one boarded the old Stark Street Ferry on the west side of Portland's Willamette River. Arriving in East Portland, the excursionist climbed aboard the two-car P&V train that was pulled by a wood-burner (this motor car was nothing more than a steam engine disguised to look like a passenger car). "The Dummy," as this curiously designed locomotive was dubbed, traveled east to Union Avenue, proceeding north on Union. It made frequent stops until it passed Russell Street, the city boundary line. Here the train left the city streets and followed its own right-of-way through Piedmont, Cloverdale and Woodlawn.

In those days, the last decade of the nineteenth century, the entire area north of Hayden Island was under water. Nearly half the river was crossed by a long trestle, at the end of which was Hayden Landing. The journey was completed by the ferry Vancouver, crossing the Columbia into Washington. The ferry remained in use until the Interstate Bridge was completed, but "The Dummy" was replaced by electric cars in July, 1893.

Time Schedule No. 9, P. and V. Railroad Company.

No.	LEAVE EAST PORTLAND.	No.	LEAVE VANCOUVER
1	*6 35 A. M.	1	*6 30 A. M.
2	8 00 A. M.	2	8 15 A. M.
3	9 20 A. M.	3	9 40 A. M.
4	10 50 A. M.	4	11 10 A. M.
5	12 10 A. M.	5	12 25 P. M.
6	1 15 P. M.	6	1 30 P. M.
7	1 55 P. M.	7	2 10 P. M.
8	2 35 P. M.	8	2 50 P. M.
9	3 15 P. M.	9	3 30 P. M.
10	3 55 P. M.	10	4 10 P. M.
11	5 15 P. M.	11	5 30 P. M.
12	6 20 P. M.	12	6 35 P. M.
13	8 55 P. M.	13	9 10 P. M.
14	11 30 P. M.	14	11 45 P. M.

*These trains do not run on Sundays.
Extra Trains Leave Woodlawn 6.15 a. m., 12.45 p. m.

Ferry VANCOUVER ready to leave from Hayden Landing for Vancouver, Washington, across the·Columbia.

Hayden Landing (Oregon Historical Society photo)

CHAPTER 24

THE EAST SIDE RAILWAY COMPANY

The ESR was a fifteen-mile electrified line that operated from Portland to Oregon City. Built in 1893, it is believed to be the first interurban line in the United States using electric current generated by water power.

As it increased its trackage in Multno-mah and Clackamas Counties, it was bought and sold a number of times. What was originally the ESR became the Oregon Water Power & Railway Company, then the Portland Railway Light & Power Company, the Portland Electric Power Company, and, lastly, the Portland Traction Company.

One of the first electrified cars to arrive in Oregon City shortly after the EAST SIDE line opened in 1893.

An EAST SIDE RAILWAY COMPANY scene in 1898 showing the elaborate railroad station built at Gladstone. The car shown here, ran from Oregon City to Gladstone and to a long spur built by the railroad into the Chautauqua Grounds making a circle trip hourly during the period of festivities. A Mr. Gault operated the car for many years. The Clackamas County National Guard are shown assembled on the station grounds.

159
EAST SIDE RAILWAY COMPANY.

C. H. PRESCOTT, RECEIVER.

Pass ...*N. E. Cooper and wife*...

On ....*All*.................... Division

Between .... and ....

Until *3" December* 1900, *unless revoked*

A. L. Maxwell

**NOT
TRANSFERABLE**   SUPERINTENDENT

PORTLAND-ESTACADA ELECTRIC TRAIN.

SEVEN DAILY TRAINS BETWEEN PORTLAND

AND

GRESHAM, ANDERSON, BORING, BARTON, EAGLE CREEK, CURRINSVILLE, ESTACADA AND CAZADERO

CARS EVERY 40 MINUTES BETWEEN PORTLAND AND OREGON CITY

FREIGHT TRAINS DAILY EXCEPT SUNDAY

MILK AND CREAM SHIPMENTS GIVEN PASSENGER TRAIN SERVICE

Ticket Office and Waiting Room, First and Alder Streets.   Freight Depot, East Water Street and Hawthorne Avenue

1905 advertising for the electric lines from Portland to Oregon City

Note the Troutdale line and the extension from Oregon City to Mount Angel has not as yet been built. (The 1905 period.)

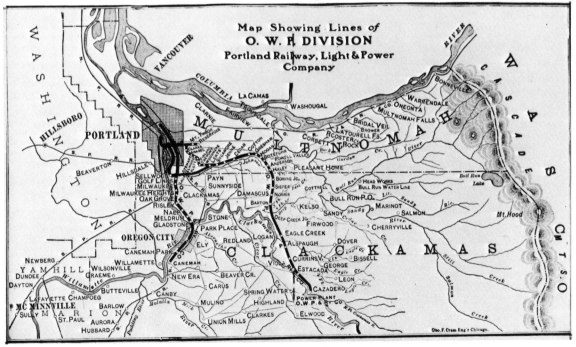

SPRINGWATER DIV OF O. W. P. RY. CO.

AT GOLF JUNCTION. SELLWOOD.

The OREGON WATER POWER & RAILWAY COMPANY scene in 1905, showing the arrival of the interurban cars at Golf Junction—located in the middle of the "Y." Cars shown here are inbound to Portland from Cazadera and Estacada. The track to the extreme right goes to Oregon City.

The Oaks amusement park opened to the general public on May 30, 1905, just two days before the Lewis & Clark Exposition got under way. The $100,000 amusement park was built by OREGON WATER POWER & RAILWAY COMPANY as a source of revenue for their railroad. The Oaks station was built on a rail line running between Portland and Oregon City. Note that in the photo, the cars on the main line are making a circle into the Oaks station getting ready for a return trip to Portland.

Cars arriving at Canemah Park, 1905. People can be seen crossing the main line track of the SP with Oregon City and the Willamette River in the background.

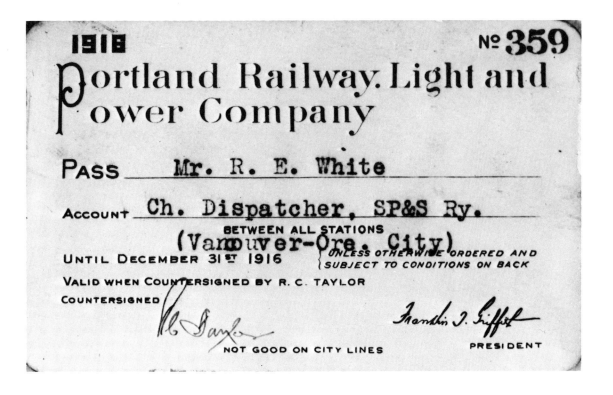

1918 № 359

Portland Railway. Light and Power Company

PASS ____Mr. R. E. White____

ACCOUNT ____Ch. Dispatcher, SP&S Ry.____

BETWEEN ALL STATIONS
(Vancouver-Ore. City)

UNTIL DECEMBER 31ST 1916 UNLESS OTHERWISE ORDERED AND SUBJECT TO CONDITIONS ON BACK

VALID WHEN COUNTERSIGNED BY R. C. TAYLOR

COUNTERSIGNED

NOT GOOD ON CITY LINES

PRESIDENT

Portland Railway, Light & Power Co.

O. W. P. DIVISION—TIME TABLE

ESTACADA-CAZADERO LINE 35 MILES

Stations	West Bound								
Cazadero Lv	......		7 30	9 30	11 30	1 30	3 40	5 30	9 00
Estacada	.....		7 37	9 37	11 37	1 37	3 47	5 37	9 05
Currinsville................	......		7 43	9 43	11 43	1 43	3 53	5 43	9 11
Alspaugh..............	......		7 46	9 46	11 46	1 46	3 56	5 46	9 14
Eagle Creek			7 49	9 49	11 49	1 49	3 59	5 49	9 17
Barton			7 55	9 55	11 55	1 55	4 05	5 55	9 23
Siefer.................			8 02	10 02	12 02	2 02	4 12	6 02	9 30
Boring ..	.....		8 05	10 05	12 05	2 05	4 15	6 05	9 33
Anderson	.....		8 11	10 11	12 11	2 11	4 21	6 11	9 39
Hogan	.....		8 16	10 16	12 16	2 16	4 26	6 16	9 44
Gresham..............		6 40	8 20	10 20	12 20	2 20	4 30	6 20	9 48
Cedarville.............		6 44	8 24	10 24	12 24	2 24	4 34	6 24	9 52
Sycamore		6 50	8 30	10 30	12 30	2 30	4 40	6 30	9 58
Lents Junction..........		6 57	8 37	10 37	12 37	2 37	4 47	6 37	10 05
Golf Junction...........			8 52	10 52	12 52	2 52	5 03	6 52	10 18
Portland ....Ar	7 45		9 10	11 10	1 10	3 10	5 27	7 10	10 38

Stations	East Bound								
Portland Lv	5.45	7 30	9 30	11 30	1 30	3 40	5 44	7 15	
Golf Junction.............	......	7 48	9 48	11 48	1 48	3 58	6 02	7 33	
Lents Junction............	6 20	8 02	10 03	12 03	2 03	4 13	6 17	7 48	
Sycamore	6 27	8 10	10 10	12 10	2 10	4 20	6 24	7 55	
Cedarville..................	6 33	8 16	10 16	12 16	2 16	4 26	6 30	8 01	
Gresham.................	6 37	8 20	10 20	12 20	2 20	4 30	6 34	8 05	
Hogan	......	8 24	10 24	12 24	2 24	4 34	6 38	8 09	
Anderson	*	8 29	10 29	12 29	2 29	4 39	6 43	8 14	
Boring		8 35	10 35	12 35	2 35	4 45	6 49	8 20	
Siefer.................		8 38	10 38	12 38	2 38	4 48	6 52	8 23	
Barton		8 45	10 45	12 45	2 45	4 55	6 59	8 30	
Eagle Creek		8 51	10 51	12 51	2 51	5 01	7 05	8 36	
Alspaugh		8 54	10 54	12 54	2 54	5 04	7 08	8 39	
Currinsville..............		8 57	10 57	12 57	2 57	5 07	7 11	8 42	
Estacada.................		9 03	11 03	1 03	3 03	5 13	7 17	8 48	
Cazadero ....Ar	....	9 10	11 10	1 10	3 10	5 20	7 24	8.53	

A. M. Figures in Roman.   P. M. Figures in Black.   *Daily except Sunday

OREGON CITY AND CANEMAH PARK 15 MILES

LV—PORTLAND				Lv—OREGON CITY AND CANEMAH			
†4 15	10 20	3 00	7 40	5 45	11 00	3 40	8 20
6 20	11 00	3 40	8 20	7 00	11 40	4 20	9 00
7 00	11 40	4 20	9 00	7 40	12 20	5 00	* 9 20
7 40	12 20	5 00	*9 20	8 20	1 00	5 40	10 00
8 20	1 00	5 40	10 00	9 00	1 40	6 20	11 00
9 00	1 40	6 20	11 00	9 40	2 20	7 00	*12 00
9 40	2 20	7 00	12 00	10 20	3 00	7 40	* 1 00

A. M. figures in Roman.   P. M. figures in black.   *Indicates to Milwaukie only.
†Via Lents Junction.

F. I. FULLER, Vice-Pres. and Gen'l Mgr.   C. J. FRANKLIN, Gen'l Superintendent
G. C. FIELDS, Superintendent   W. P. MULCHAY, Traffic Agent

Timetable for 1905

This was the end of the Estacada interurban line running from Portland. PRL&P No. 1040 Motor awaits the necessary time before leaving for the return trip to Portland.

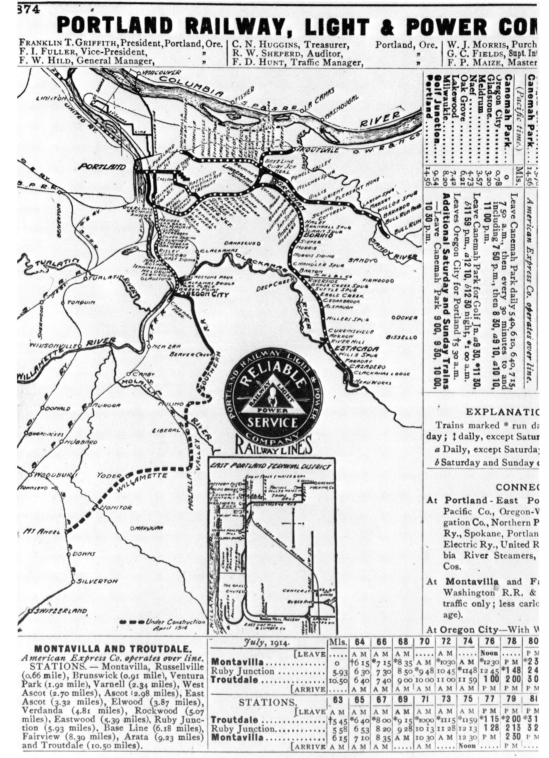

374

PORTLAND RAILWAY, LIGHT & POWER COM[PANY]

FRANKLIN T. GRIFFITH, President, Portland, Ore. | C. N. HUGGINS, Treasurer,   Portland, Ore. | W. J. MORRIS, Purch[asing]
F. I. FULLER, Vice-President,   „ | R. W. SHEPERD, Auditor,   „ | G. C. FIELDS, Supt. In[...]
F. W. HILD, General Manager,   „ | F. D. HUNT, Traffic Manager,   „ | F. P. MAIZE, Master [...]

Canemah Park.		
(Pacific time.)		
Canemah Park.	Mls.	14.56
Oregon City.	0	
Gladstone.	0.78	
Meldrum.	3.20	
Naef.	3.57	
Oak Grove.	4.73	
Lakewood.	6.21	
Milwaukie.	7.42	
Golf Junction.	8.20	
Portland.	9.54	
	14.56	

American Express Co. operates over line.

Leave Canemah Park daily 5 40, 6 10, 6 40, 7 15, including 7 50 a.m., then every 30 minutes to and 11 00 p.m.
Leave Canemah Park for Golf Jn. *a*9 30, *a*11 50, *b*11 59 p.m., *a*12 10, *b*12 30 night, *1 00 a.m.
Leaves Oregon City for Portland ‡5 30 a.m.
—Additional Saturday and Sunday Trains Leave Canemah Park 9 00, 9 30, 10 00.
Leave Canemah Park 10 30 p.m.

EXPLANATIO[N]

Trains marked * run da[ily except Sun]day; ‡ daily, except Satur[day...]
a Daily, except Saturday [...]
b Saturday and Sunday o[nly...]

CONNEC[TIONS]

At Portland - East Po[rtland...]
Pacific Co., Oregon-W[ashington Navi]gation Co., Northern P[acific]
Ry., Spokane, Portland [& Seattle]
Electric Ry., United R[ailways, Colum]bia River Steamers, [...]
Cos.

At Montavilla and F[airview—Oregon]
Washington R.R. & [Navigation Co.,]
traffic only; less carlo[ad lots (stor]age).

At Oregon City—With W[...]

MONTAVILLA AND TROUTDALE.
American Express Co. operates over line.
STATIONS. — Montavilla, Russellville (0.66 mile), Brunswick (0.91 mile), Ventura Park (1.92 mile), Varnell (2.34 miles), West Ascot (2.70 miles), Ascot (2.98 miles), East Ascot (3.32 miles), Elwood (3.87 miles), Verdanda (4.81 miles), Rockwood (5.07 miles), Eastwood (5.39 miles), Ruby Junction (5.93 miles), Base Line (6.18 miles), Fairview (8.39 miles), Arata (9.23 miles) and Troutdale (10.50 miles).

July, 1914.		Mls.	64	66	68	70	72	74	76	78	80
	[LEAVE	.....	A M	A M	A M		A M		Noon		P M
Montavilla		0	†6 15	*7 15	*8 35		*10 30	A M	*12 30	P M	*2 3[0]
Ruby Junction		5.93	6 30	7 30	8 50	*9 48	10 45	*11 48	12 45	*1 48	2 4[8]
Troutdale		10.50	6 40	7 40	9 00	10 00	11 00	11 59	1 00	2 00	3 0[0]
	[ARRIVE		A M	A M	A M	A M	A M	A M	P M	P M	P M
STATIONS.		63	65	67	69	71	73	75	77	79	81
	[LEAVE	A M	A M	A M	A M	A M	A M	A M	P M	P M	P M
Troutdale		†5 45	*6 40	*8 00	*9 15	*10 00	*11 15	*11 59	*1 15	*2 00	*3 1[5]
Ruby Junction		5 58	6 53	8 20	9 28	10 13	11 28	12 13	1 28	2 13	3 2[8]
Montavilla		6 15	7 10	8 35	A M	10 30	A M	12 30	P M	2 30	P M
	[ARRIVE	A M	A M	A M		A M		Noon		P M	

BETWEEN PORTLAND AND BULL RUN AND CAZADERO.—*American Express Co. operates o[ver...]*

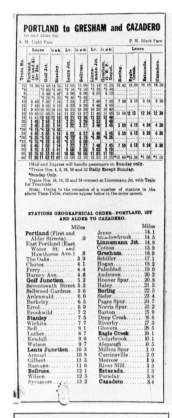

PORTLAND to GRESHAM and CAZADERO
1st and Alder Sts.
A. M. Light Face. P. M. Black Face.

1 Mail and Express will handle passengers on Sunday only.
*Trains Nos. 4, 8, 26, 30 and 32 Daily Except Sunday.
†Sunday Only.
Trains Nos. 10, 16, 22 and 34 connect at Linnemann Jct. with Train for Troutdale.
Note: Owing to the omission of a number of stations in the above Time-Table, stations appear below in the order named.

STATIONS GEOGRAPHICAL ORDER—PORTLAND, 1ST AND ALDER TO CAZADERO.

Station	Miles	Station	Miles
Portland (First and Alder Streets)	.0	Jenne	14.1
East Portland (East Water St. and Hawthorne Ave.)	.8	Meadowbrook	14.5
		Linnemann Jct.	14.8
		Cotton	15.9
		Gresham	16.9
The Oaks	3.9	Schiller	17.1
Chutes	4.1	Hogan	18.2
Ferry	4.4	Palmblad	19.0
Harney Ave.	4.6	Anderson	20.2
Golf Junction	5.2	Hoover Spur	20.8
Seventeenth Street	5.3	Haley	21.5
Sellwood Gardens	5.6	Boring	22.5
Ardenwald	6.0	Siefer	23.4
Berkeley	6.5	Pages Spur	24.7
Errol	6.9	Norris Spur	25.2
Brookwild	7.2	Barton	25.9
Stanley	7.5	Deep Creek	26.6
Wichita	7.7	Riverby	27.3
Bell	8.1	Glovers	28.5
Luther	8.7	Eagle Creek	29.1
Kendall	9.0	Cedarbrook	30.1
Watson	9.7	Alspaugh	30.5
Lents Junction	10.3	Millers Spur	31.0
Arnaud	10.8	Currinsville	32.0
Gilbert	11.3	Morrow	32.9
Ramapo	11.6	River Mill	33.3
Bellrose	12.1	Estacada	33.3
Wilson	12.5	Faraday	33.8
Sycamore	13.2	Cazadero	34

CAZADERO and GRESHAM to PORTLAND
1st and Alder Sts.
A. M. Light Face. P. M. Black Face.

Note: *Trains Nos. *1, *3, *7, *23, *29 and *31; Daily Except Sunday.
†Train No. 1301 Sunday only.

Special Sunday Excursion Fares to

Bull Run **75c** Estacada
Round Trip

Purchase Tickets Before Boarding Trains

Canemah Park
(Take Oregon City Trains)
Dancing Every Sunday Evening

Crystal Lake Park
(Take Oregon City Trains)
Picnics, Swimming, Dancing Every Sunday

Cedarville Park
(Take Estacada or Bull Run Trains)
Ideal Picnic Grounds

For further information call
Ticket Agent, First and Alder Streets,
Marshall 5, A 6131

MAY 26, 1917

"THE TROUT ROUTE"

PORTLAND RAILWAY LIGHT AND POWER COMPANY

TIME TABLE

INTERURBAN LINES

AMERICAN EXPRESS COMPANY OPERATES OVER THIS COMPANY'S LINES

SUBJECT TO CHANGE WITHOUT NOTICE

F. D. HUNT, TRAFFIC MANAGER G. C. FIELDS, SUPERINTENDENT

GENERAL OFFICES
ELECTRIC BUILDING, ALDER AT BROADWAY
PORTLAND, OREGON

PORTLAND to GRESHAM and BULL RUN
1st and Alder Sts.
A. M. Light Face. P. M. Black Face.

*Daily Except Sunday. †Sunday only.

GEOGRAPHICAL LIST OF STATIONS
Portland, 1st and Alder to Bull Run.

Station	Miles	Station	Miles
Portland (First and Alder Streets)	.0	Ramapo	11.6
East Portland (East Water St. and Hawthorne Ave.)	.8	Bellrose	12.1
		Wilson	12.5
		Sycamore	13.2
The Oaks	3.9	Jenne	14.1
Chutes	4.2	Meadowbrook	14.5
Ferry	4.4	Linnemann Jct.	14.8
Harney Ave.	4.6	Brunner	16.1
Golf Junction	5.2	Ruby Junction	16.6
Seventeenth Street	5.3	Neal	17.5
Sellwood Gardens	5.6	Gresham	18.4
Ardenwald	6.0	Powell Valley	19.8
Berkeley	6.5	Gustavus	20.4
Errol	6.9	Welches Spur	21.2
Brookwild	7.2	Gillis	22.1
Stanley	7.5	Orient	23.1
Wichita	7.7	Pleasant Home	23.8
Bell	8.1	Scenic	24.3
Luther	8.7	Cottrell	25.4
Kendall	9.0	Mabery	27.2
Watson	9.7	Baraboo	29.1
Lents Junction	10.3	Bull Run Park	24.5
Arnaud	10.8	Cameron Spur	29.8
Gilbert	11.3	Bull Run	30.8

BULL RUN and GRESHAM to PORTLAND
1st and Alder Sts.
A. M. Light Face. P. M. Black Face.

FISHING STREAMS
Sandy River and Bull Run River—Here may be found the finest streams and beauty spots along our lines. Bull Run Park is at the confluence of the Bull Run and Big and Little Sandy Rivers. Aside from the fishing the picturesque and rugged scenery is well worth the day's outing.

MONTAVILLA-LINNEMANN to TROUTDALE
Mt. Hood Depot.

Montavilla-Linnemann Jct. to Troutdale	Troutdale to Montavilla-Linnemann Jct.

*Daily except Sunday. A. M. figures in light face. P. M. figures in black face.

Note: Take Montavilla City car at 3rd and Yamhill, marked Mt. Hood Depot on dash sign, allow 50 minutes to Mt. Hood Station at Montavilla. Also trains leaving 1st and Alder on Estacada Line at 6.45, 10.45 A. M., 2.45 and 6.45 P. M. connect at Linnemann Jct. for Fairview, Troutdale and intermediate stations.

LIST OF STATIONS GEOGRAPHICAL ORDER
Montavilla to Troutdale

Station	Miles	Station	Miles
Montavilla	.0	Hope	5.0
Russellville	.6	Eastwood	5.3
Brunswick	.9	Ruby Jct.	5.9
Nendel	1.2	Base Line	6.2
Ventura Park	1.9	Baird's Dale	7.2
Varnel	2.3	Osburn	7.5
West Ascot	2.7	Cleone	8.1
Ascot	2.9	Fairview	8.4
East Ascot	3.2	Arata	9.2
Elwood	3.8	Multnomah Farm	9.7
Verdanta	4.4	Keady	10.0
Rockwood	4.8	Troutdale	10.5

Excursion and Outing

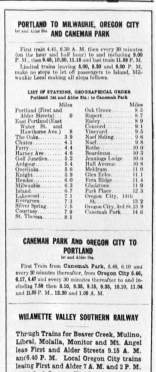

PORTLAND TO MILWAUKIE, OREGON CITY AND CANEMAH PARK
1st and Alder Sts.

First train 4.41, 6.30 A. M. then every 30 minutes (on the hour and half hour) to and including 9.00 P. M., then 9.45, 10.30, 11.15 and last train 11.59 P. M. Limited trains leaving 5.00, 5.30 and 6.00 P. M. make no stops to let off passengers to Island, Milwaukie Local making all stops follows.

LIST OF STATIONS, GEOGRAPHICAL ORDER
Portland (1st and Alder Sts.) to Canemah Park

Station	Miles	Station	Miles
Portland (First and Alder Streets)	.0	Oak Grove	8.3
East Portland (East Water St. and Hawthorne Ave.)	.8	Rupert	8.7
		Risley	8.9
		Concord	9.1
The Oaks	3.9	Vineyard	9.5
Chutes	4.1	Naef Siding	9.6
Ferry	4.4	Naef	9.8
Harney Ave.	4.6	Rothe	10.0
Golf Junction	5.2	Boardman	10.3
Ardgour	5.4	Jennings Lodge	10.6
Overlinks	5.6	Hull Avenue	10.8
Knight	5.9	Meldrum	11.0
Hendee	6.0	Glen Echo	11.1
Milwaukie	6.3	Fern Ridge	11.4
Island	6.7	Gladstone	11.9
Lakewood	7.1	Park Place	12.3
Evergreen	7.3	Oregon City, 14th	
Silver Spring	7.5	St.	13.2
Courtney	7.9	Oregon City, 3rd St.	13.9
St. Theresa	8.1	Canemah Park	14.6

CANEMAH PARK AND OREGON CITY TO PORTLAND
1st and Alder Sts.

First Train from Canemah Park, 5.40, 6.10 and every 30 minutes thereafter, from Oregon City 5.46, 6.17, 6.47 and every 30 minutes thereafter to and including 7.58 then 8.10, 8.35, 9.15, 9.35, 10.10, 11.04 and 11.30 P. M., 12.30 and 1.05 A. M.

WILLAMETTE VALLEY SOUTHERN RAILWAY

Through Trains for Beaver Creek, Mulino, Liberal, Molalla, Monitor and Mt. Angel leave First and Alder Streets 9.15 A. M. and 6.40 P. M. Local Oregon City trains leaving First and Alder 7 A. M. and 2 P. M. connect at Oregon City for above points. For rates, etc., call Ticket Agent P. R. L. & Co.—Mar. 5100—A 6131.

PORTLAND RAILWAY LIGHT & POWER COMPANY stations about 1917. *Above*, Jennings Lodge; *below*, Boring.

A Cazadero car from Portland stops at Linneman Junction for a connection with the stub train to Troutdale, 1920.

1930   No. A **249**

PORTLAND ELECTRIC POWER COMPANY

Pass   Mr R E White--
       Dispatcher

Account   Spokane Portland & Seattle Ry Co

BETWEEN ALL STATIONS

UNTIL DECEMBER 31, 1930, UNLESS OTHERWISE ORDERED
AND SUBJECT TO CONDITIONS ON BACK

VALID WHEN COUNTERSIGNED BY A. QUINN

COUNTERSIGNED

                                          PRESIDENT

NOT GOOD ON CITY LINES

PORTLAND ELECTRIC POWER COMPANY car at Gresham in 1932

A PORTLAND TRACTION COMPANY car at Evergreen in 1958. This picture was taken short-ly before all passenger service was discontinued on the entire railroad.

CHAPTER 25

WILLAMETTE VALLEY
SOUTHERN RAILWAY COMPANY

A thirty-five mile electrified line built in 1915 from Oregon City to Mt. Angel, the WVSR connected with the Portland Railway Light & Power Company at Oregon City. (The PRL&P ran from Portland to Oregon City.) The line was financed by farmers and investors in Clackamas and Marion Counties.

The original plan for the WVSR was to build through to Salem. But when construction actually began, the terminus was changed to Silverton. The plan was to connect with the Silver Falls Timber Company, a public carrier rail line operating their own logging trains, some 1,000 cars of lumber annually, into transcontinental territory. The Silver Falls Timber Company, although connecting with the Southern Pacific at Silverton, encouraged a second railroad. The additional line would give them more of the much-needed boxcars during the peak car-shortage periods, which had plagued the Pacific Northwest for many years.

Although construction began with great anticipation, the line was only able to reach Mt. Angel. The line's president, Grant Dimick, tried unsuccessfully to se-

cure loans to carry on the work, but after serious financial setbacks, the PRL&P took over the line, renaming it the Willamette Valley Railway. The connection

WILLAMETTE VALLEY SOUTHERN RAILWAY

TIME TABLE No. 15
Effective April 1, 1926

PORTLAND TO MOLALLA

STATIONS	2 Daily A.M.	4 Daily A.M.	6 Daily A.M.	8 Daily P.M.	10 Daily P.M.	12 Daily P.M.
Portland (1st and Alder)........Lv.	6.30	8.15	10.00	1.00	3.00	5.00
Oregon City......	7.20	9.05	11.10	1.45	3.45	5.45
Buena Vista......	7.22	9.07	11.12	1.47	3.47	5.47
Collis...........	7.24	9.09	11.14	1.49	3.49	5.49
Campine.........	7.25	9.10	11.15	1.50	3.50	5.50
McBain..........	7.28	9.13	11.18	1.53	3.53	5.53
Maple Lane......	7.31	9.17	11.22	1.57	3.57	5.57
Robbins..........	7.32	9.18	11.23	1.58	3.58	5.58
Glen Oak........	7.34	9.20	11.25	2.00	4.00	6.00
Swift............	7.35	9.21	11.26	2.01	4.01	6.01
Eby.............	7.37	9.24	11.29	2.04	4.03	6.03
Beaver Creek.....s	7.38	9.25	11.30	2.05	4.05	6.05
Ingram...........	7.41	9.28	11.33	2.08	4.08	6.08
Spangler.........	7.43	9.30	11.35	2.10	4.10	6.10
Lewis............	7.44	9.31	11.36	2.11	4.11	6.11
Buckner Creek....	7.50	9.37	11.42	2.17	4.17	6.17
Howard..........	7.53	9.40	11.45	2.20	4.20	6.20
Mulino..........s	7.55	9.42	11.47	2.22	4.22	6.22
North Liberal....	7.59	9.46	11.51	2.26	4.26	6.26
Liberal..........	8.00	9.48	11.53	2.28	4.28	6.28
Huntley..........	8.01	9.49	11.54	2.29	4.29	6.29
Richard..........	8.03	9.51	11.56	2.31	4.31	6.31
Molalla..........	8.05	9.55	12.00	2.35	4.35	6.35

s—Stops.
All other stations trains will stop upon flag only.
A.M. figures in light face.
P.M. figures in **black face.**

A view of the WVS railroad station in Oregon City. This was an old converted family home located in the center of town.

allowed through electric interurban service from Mt. Angel to Portland. However, in 1933 the line was abandoned.

WILLAMETTE VALLEY SOUTHERN RAILWAY COMPANY

TRIP PASS   No. 901
SUBJECT TO CONDITIONS ON BACK

_____1927
PASS_____
Account_____
From _____
To _____
Good for One Trip Until_____1927
Address_____ Requested by_____
Valid When Countersigned by_____
COUNTERSIGNED
                                              PRESIDENT
_____
              NOT GOOD ON CITY LINES

Unloading Henry's latest 1915 Model T Fords at Oregon City. These automobiles just arrived from Detroit, Michigan. The WVS station can be seen in the background.

At Spangler station an interurban WVS car, No. 1, holds the main while the "way freight" goes "in the hole."

Here at Beaver Creek, an electrified motor is pulling an "Extra Freight" enroute Mt. Angel

Mt. Angel marked the end of the thirty-one mile line for the WVS. This is a small Catholic community—the spire of their church can be seen above the station.

CHAPTER 26

THE OREGON ELECTRIC RAILWAY
The Willamette Valley Route

In western Oregon will be found the famous Willamette Valley, sixty miles wide and 150 long, with few equals anywhere on earth for fruitfulness and productivity. This was the "Promised Land" for the early pioneers who crossed the continent in search of a better place to live. And through the center of this valley the Oregon Electric Railway ran its 122 miles of trackage from Portland to Eugene.

Enthusiasm for the electric or "juice line," which draws its power from an overhead cable, hit the country like a storm during the first decade of the twentieth century. The electric railways advertised "No soot—No cinders," a statement that the old steam engine could not equal. The Oregon Electric probably spawned more variety in station design and style than any other single Railway, some of which can be found in the following pages.

The ticket office and waiting room were used the last few years before the railroad discontinued passenger service down the valley. The Hawthorne Bridge crossing the Willamette River can be seen in the background. Jefferson Street Terminal. (1930)

OE No. 33—a two car train ready to roll for Eugene. The crew as shown from left to right: Milo C. Mathews, Brakeman; James M. Bilbrey, Conductor; George Laseiur, expressman; and Joe Halley, Engineer.

This photograph, taken in 1912, shows hop pickers getting ready to board the OREGON ELECTRIC at Jefferson Street Terminal in Portland. The train took them into the valley. The farmers generally offered the pickers small cottages to live in, but the pickers brought their own bedding and personal needs.

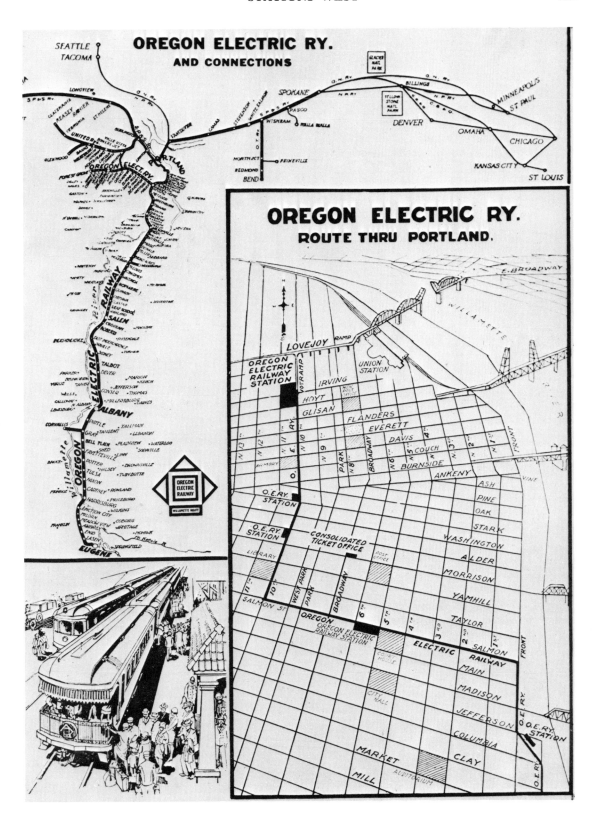

UNITED RAILWAYS CO.

PORTLAND, LINNTON, BURLINGTON, NORTH PLAINS AND WILKESBORO TRAINS

LEAVE PORTLAND	ARRIVE PORTLAND
8.15 A. M.............10.15 A. M.	7.55 A. M.............12.25 P. M.
1.15 P. M.............6.15 P. M.	2.55 P. M.............5.55 P. M.

PORTLAND, LINNTON, BURLINGTON TRAINS

LEAVE PORTLAND	ARRIVE PORTLAND
6.15 A. M...7.15 A. M...9.15 A. M.	8.55 A. M...9.55 A. M...10.55 A. M.
11.15 A. M...2.15 P. M...3.15 P. M.	1.55 P. M...3.55 P. M...4.55 P. M.
4.15 P. M.	

PORTLAND, LINNTON TRAINS

LEAVE PORTLAND	ARRIVE PORTLAND
7.45 P. M.............11.35 P. M.	6.55 A. M.......(Except Sunday)
(Sat. and Sun. only).10.00 P. M.	6.55 P. M...7.35 P. M...11.25 P.M.
	12.45 A. M.
	(Sat. and Sun. only)..9.50 P. M.

All trains run daily except as noted. Trains stop regularly at Linnton, Burlington and North Plains, and on signal at all other points.

Portland time shown is at station, Second and Stark Streets. Stops are also made at the following start intersections: 5th and Stark, 10th and Stark, 12th and Burnside, 12th and Glisan.

ROUND TRIPS EAST

On the dates given below, round trip tickets will be sold from Portland to the points in the East shown below, and many others, at the greatly reduced fares quoted: From Salem, $1.50, Forest Grove, 75 cts., Hillsboro, 60 cts. Higher, and other points on the Oregon Electric Ry. at proportional fares.

Through tickets are sold by agents of Oregon Electric Ry. in connection with The North Bank Road, Northern Pacific and Great Northern Rys. No change of Stations in Portland. Through trains from Portland.

ATLANTIC CITY,	$111.00	BALTIMORE,	$107.50
BOSTON,	110.60	BUFFALO,	91.50
CHICAGO,	72.50	COLORADO SPRINGS,	55.00
DENVER,	55.00	DETROIT,	82.50
DULUTH,	60.00	KANSAS CITY,	60.00
MILWAUKEE,	72.50	MINNEAPOLIS,	60.00
MONTREAL,	105.00	NEW YORK,	108.50
OMAHA,	60.00	PHILADELPHIA,	108.50
PITTSBURG,	91.50	ST. LOUIS,	70.00
ST. PAUL,	60.00	TORONTO,	91.50
WASHINGTON,	107.50		

DATES OF SALE

JUNE, 6, 7, 8, 13, 14, 15, 17, 18, 19, 20, 21, 24, 25, 27, 28, 29, 1912.
JULY 2, 3, 6, 7, 11, 12, 15, 16, 20, 22, 23, 26, 29, 30, 31, 1912.
AUGUST, 1, 2, 3, 6, 7, 12, 15, 16, 22, 23, 29, 30, 31, 1912.
SEPTEMBER, 4, 5, 6, 7, 8, 11, 12, 30, 1912.

Stopovers and choice of routes allowed in each direction, Final return limit October 31, 1912.

Details of schedules, fares, etc., will be furnished by agents.

JUNE 7, 1912

OREGON ELECTRIC RAILWAY

WILLAMETTE ROUTE
AND
UNITED RAILWAYS

TRAIN SCHEDULES

PORTLAND PASSENGER STATIONS

OREGON ELECTRIC RY.

THE NORTH BANK STATION, ELEVENTH AND HOYT STREETS
JEFFERSON ST. STATION, FRONT AND JEFFERSON STS.

UNITED RAILWAYS

STARK AND SECOND STS.

SALEM PASSENGER STATION

HIGH AND MILL STREETS

PORTLAND CITY TICKET OFFICES

FIFTH AND STARK STS.
JONES DRUG CO., 10TH AND STARK STS.
LELAND DRUG CO., 10TH AND MORRISON STS.

W. E. COMAN

GENERAL FREIGHT AND PASSENGER AGENT

PORTLAND, OREGON

SUBJECT TO CHANGE WITHOUT NOTICE

12-C   101950

Oregon Electric Ry.

CHANGES
IN
Passenger Train Service

Effective Sunday, July 24, the Oregon Electric Ry. will discontinue all passenger trains except Nos. 9 and 12.

The following is a condensed schedule of these trains on and after above date:

No. 9 Daily	Jefferson Street	No. 12 Daily
8.45 a.m.	Lv..........Portland.........Ar.	5.30 p.m.
9.03 a.m.	Ar......Garden Home......Lv.	5.12 p.m.
9.15 a.m.	Ar..........Tualatin.........Lv.	4.57 p.m.
10.15 a.m.	Ar..........Salem..........Lv.	4.00 p.m.
10.55 a.m.	Ar..........Albany.........Lv.	3.20 p.m.
11.25 a.m.	Ar.........*Corvallis.........Lv.	2.50 p.m.
10.25 a.m.	Lv.........*Corvallis.........Ar.	3.50 p.m.
11.39 a.m.	Ar......Junction City......Lv.	2.36 p.m.
12.01 p.m.	Ar..........Eugene.........Lv.	2.15 p.m.

*Stage connections via Albany.
These trains will make the same stops as at present.

Oregon Electric Ry.

An Oregon Electric Railway car poster, 1932

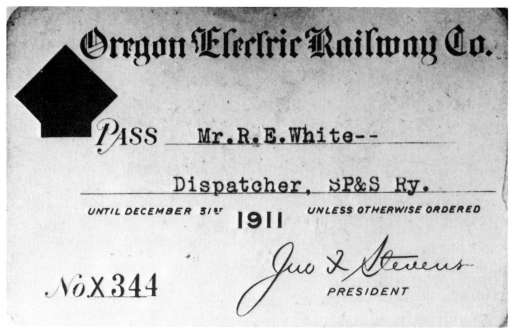

An inside view of an OREGON ELECTRIC car used in the Willamette Valley until the last trip was made in May 1933.

Garden Home was a junction for the OE trains from Portland. The track to the left goes to Salem; the track to the right goes to Forest Grove. The OE was one of the pioneer electric interurban railways in Oregon. The first fifty miles of main line, from Portland to Salem, was opened to passenger traffic in January, 1908, and to freight traffic in July of the same year. The Forest Grove division leaving the main line at Garden Home, seven miles from Portland and continuing twenty-one miles to Forest Grove, was opened to passenger traffic in October, 1908. This photograph was taken in 1909.

This station with the general store as shown is typical of many built along the line. The small under cover waiting room, open to the elements but a protection against the rains, was frequently used. Note the general store opposite the station, handling groceries, dry goods, notions, etc. The OE encouraged individuals to build these general stores, hoping that the population would follow the railroad. As a further incentive, a commission was allowed on all rail tickets sold. In this particular instance at Broadacres, Mr. J. M. Foulds, owner of the store, also became the first postmaster. This all started shortly after the first train began operating between Portland and Eugene.

Forest Grove

This photograph shows downtown Woodburn. There was no railroad station here, as tickets were sold in the local drug store. (1910)

The track passes through the very center of the French Prairie area—a section of the Willamette Valley. It is here that retired Hudson's Bay Company employees settled after serving at Fort Vancouver under Dr. John McLoughlin, the chief factor. These French-Canadians took up farming here because of the fine soil. West Woodburn is one of the earliest settlements in the state of Oregon. The city of Woodburn was served by OE from West Woodburn via a two-mile branch line into the city. Those responsible for building the OE insisted that the line be built almost entirely with straight track and this did not allow for operating the main line through a close-by city unless it was directly intermediate. Shown here is West Woodburn.

Salem, Oregon, State and High Streets, 1909. The OREGON ELECTRIC stops in front of the Hotel Salem. This hotel was the former residence of William Holden Willson who came to Oregon as one of the early Methodist missionaries and was one of the city's founders.

This station is located in the very heart of the Willamette Valley. In the background there are several barn like structures with cupolas extending up into the air. These are hop and prune dryers. Raising hops was big business in the 1910 period. Many excursion trains were operated during the season bringing vast numbers of people from Portland down the valley to help harvest the hops. It was both fun and profitable for the individual.

This attractive but small chalet-type of non-agency station offered real and unusual charm. It was a different type of railroad station than anything that had formerly appeared in Oregon. This photograph was taken in 1915.

This community lies in a farming area. Today Harrisburg ships some 400 carloads of ryegrass seed into the southeastern part of the United States. This commodity is used as a cover crop for farm areas. This photo was taken in 1910.

People used the railroad for the nine mile trip from Portland to Beaverton. Today the station would be located in the very heart of the city. Freeways, buildings, homes and industrial complexes flood the landscape today. The city and the general area are two of the fastest growing sections of Oregon. This photo was taken in 1912.

The OE reached Albany July 4, 1912. The station is shown here under construction. It is walled with brick and covered with a tile roof; it cost more than $32,000 before the structure was completed.

This photo shows the interior of the Albany station when it was new. The running time via the OREGON ELECTRIC from Portland to Albany was two hours and thirty-five minutes. Today the tracks are gone and the building is used by the American Legion.

A house-like type of railroad station. This afforded living quarters for the agent and his family as well as a small waiting room and ticket office for the public. Note the letters "OE" on the side of the station. A warehouse and a sub-power station can be seen in the background of this 1918 photograph taken at East Independence.

This sub-power station also served as a ticket office along the line

An OE train leaving Eugene for Portland

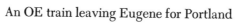

This OE station was built shortly after the railroad reached Eugene in 1912. This photograph was taken in 1914.

This 1927 photo shows the second and more deluxe station which was built in the early 1920s. The "OWL" trains running between Portland—Salem—Eugene would have their berths ready for occupancy at 9:30 P.M., even though the train didn't leave until 1:30 A.M. The "OWL" would meander along at night on a no-hurry schedule setting out a sleeper at Salem, Albany and Eugene. The business man could remain in his berth until 8 A.M., get in a day's work and then return to Portland on another "OWL" under the same conditions. Eugene Station, both pictures.

Box Motor No. 40 at the Eugene freight station getting ready to leave for the return trip to Portland. This is a 1928 photo.

CHAPTER 27

The UNITED RAILWAYS COMPANY operated twenty-eight miles of interurban electrified service from Portland to Wilkesboro in 1909. This 1915 photograph shows the Wilkesboro station built up on a piling. Electric Motor No. 3 is ready for the return trip to Portland. At this time Wilkesboro was the end of the line. Trackage was later extended to Keasey and operated under the name PORTLAND ASTORIA & PACIFIC RAILWAY COMPANY. Eventually both lines were purchased by James J. Hill and operated by SPOKANE PORTLAND & SEATTLE RAILWAY COMPANY.

Portland to Linnton . . . . via Spokane Portland & Seattle Railway
Linnton to Wilkesboro . . . . via United Railways Company
Wilkesboro to Keasey . . . . via Portland Astoria & Pacific Railway

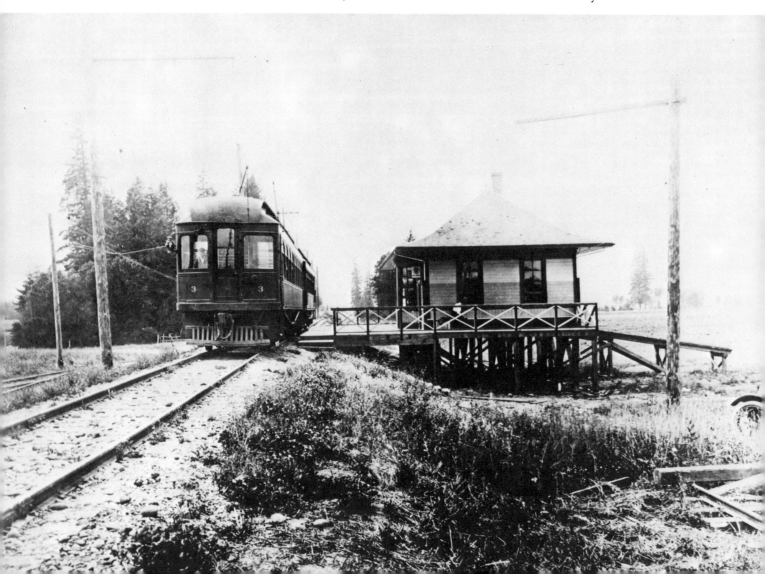

UNITED RAILWAYS

Second and Stark Streets, Portland

1912

25 Daily	15 Daily	11 Daily	7 Daily	STATIONS	4 Daily	12 Daily	16 Daily	22 Daily
6 15	1 15	10 15	8 15	Lv... Portland ...Ar.	7 55	12 25	2 55	5 55
6 50	1 50	10 50	8 51	......Linnton	7 18	11 50	2 18	5 18
7 05	2 06	11 05	9 06	.....Burlington.....	7 06	11 37	2 06	5 06
7 33	2 33	11 34	9 37	....North Plains....	6 37	11 07	1 37	4 37
7 50	2 50	11 50	10 00	Ar ..Wilkesboro .Lv.	6 20	10 50	1 20	4 20

ADDITIONAL TRAINS

Leave Portland daily 6:15, 7:15, 9:15, 11:15 A. M., 2:15, 3:15, 4:15 P. M. for Burlington and intermediate points and arrive Portland from these points 8:55, 9:55, 10:55 A. M., 1:55, 3:55 P. M.

This 1912 photograph shows a UNITED RAILWAYS train ready for boarding

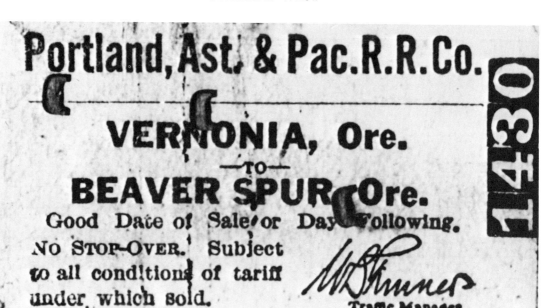

North Plains

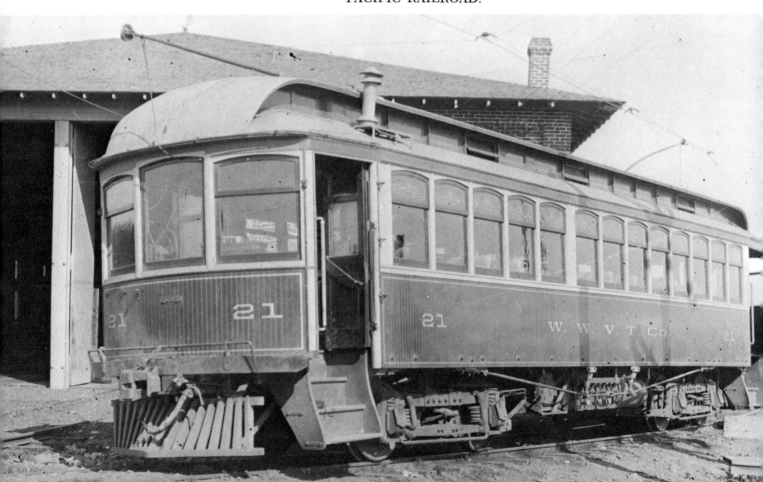

WALLA WALLA VALLEY RAILWAY COMPANY
INTERURBAN DIVISION
1912

PASS ------ Mr. H. W. Conard ------

Chief Clerk to President

ACCOUNT The Colorado Midland Ry. Co.

BETWEEN   All Stations

UNTIL DECEMBER 31, 1912, UNLESS OTHERWISE ORDERED,
AND SUBJECT TO CONDITIONS ON BACK

No. 78

GENERAL MANAGER

The WALLA WALLA VALLEY TRACTION COMPANY maintains and operates about twenty-four miles of track (only five miles of it are in the state of Oregon). The line runs from Walla Walla, Washington, to Milton, Oregon. This 1905 photograph shows Interurban Car No. 21 stopped in front of the station and carsheds at Milton. The line is now owned by NORTHERN PACIFIC RAILROAD.

GALES CREEK & WILSON RIVER RAILROAD Engine No. 1. This small twelve-mile lumber line operated from Wilkesboro to Glenwood. It was purchased by Hill Lines in 1922 and abandoned in 1929.

CHAPTER 28

THE ORIGINS OF THE
PORTLAND EUGENE &
EASTERN RAILWAY (SP)

There is an important difference between streetcars and interurban lines. Streetcars operate within the confines of one town, giving local street-by-street service. An interurban line extends from one urban community to another. Like the streetcar, it runs over city streets. However, when it reaches outlying areas it uses private right-of-way, often operating at high speeds and making stops at crossings and stations where requested.

Alvadore Welch, an electrical engineer employed by one of the large power companies in Oregon, dreamed of operating an electrified railroad from Portland to areas in California, the coast and through the Santiam Canyon with connections to several undisclosed points.

West Linn, Salem, Albany and Eugene had streetcar service that Welch needed badly for ingress into these cities. At last he was able to purchase all four lines, which gave him the most important link in the construction of his line to California. He called these collected lines the Portland Eugene & Eastern Railway Company.

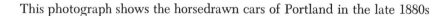

This photograph shows the horsedrawn cars of Portland in the late 1880s

Another view of Portland but showing the electrified cars of the early 1920s

A repair train stopping at Dayton, Oregon, in 1915

An electric Forest Grove car, 1908

A horsedrawn car of the 1890s in Astoria

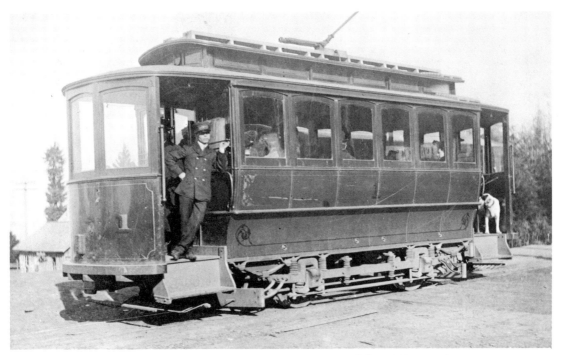

This view of Astoria shows an electric car of the 1910 period

In these early years of the twentieth century the railroads from Portland to California and from Portland east were owned by Edward Henry Harriman. When Harriman learned of Welch's plans, he became apprehensive about a rival line south. He felt, too, that if an electric line was needed, he must be the one to build it. With little difficulty he purchased the heavily mortgaged lines of Mr. Welch. The electrified line south was never built. First Harriman, then the Southern Pacific, operated the existing electric lines of the PEE as long as the traffic warranted.

An early electric trolley. This photograph was taken in Salem, 1889

The horsedrawn car of the 1890s was replaced with a steam dummey (pulling the same car) about the turn of the century. Then progress brought the small steam engine pulling one railroad passenger car. And this was followed by an electric car.

A horsedrawn car of the 1890s is shown here in front of the Occidental Hotel. Corvallis never had electrified street car service.

Electrified cars shown on the Fourth of July, 1912, at the SP Railroad Station in Eugene

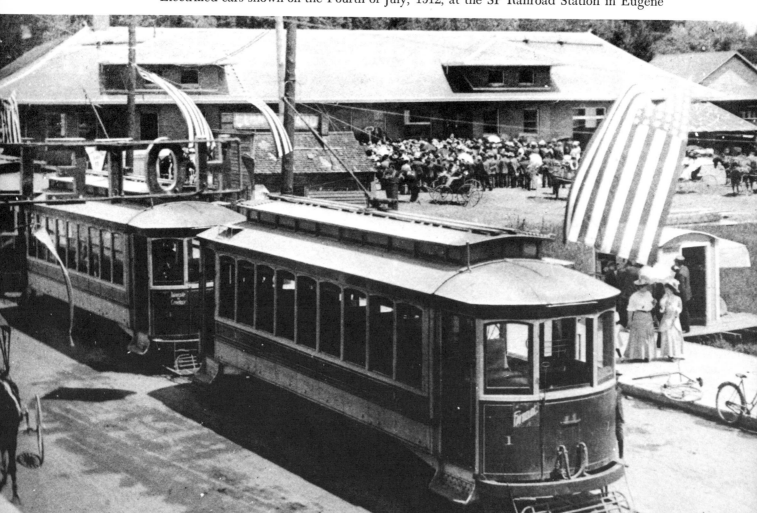

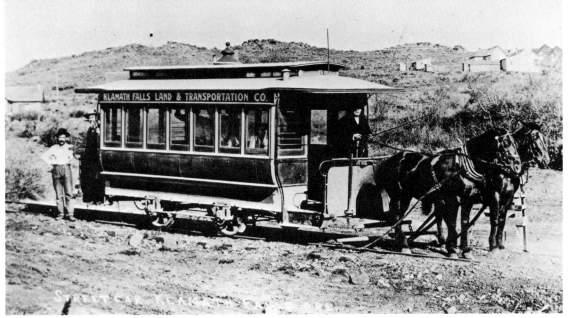

This horsedrawn car was called a "Linkville Trolley" because it was named for the town of Link-ville. This photo was taken in 1906.

This horsedrawn line operated for a year or so; it was never replaced by an electric line

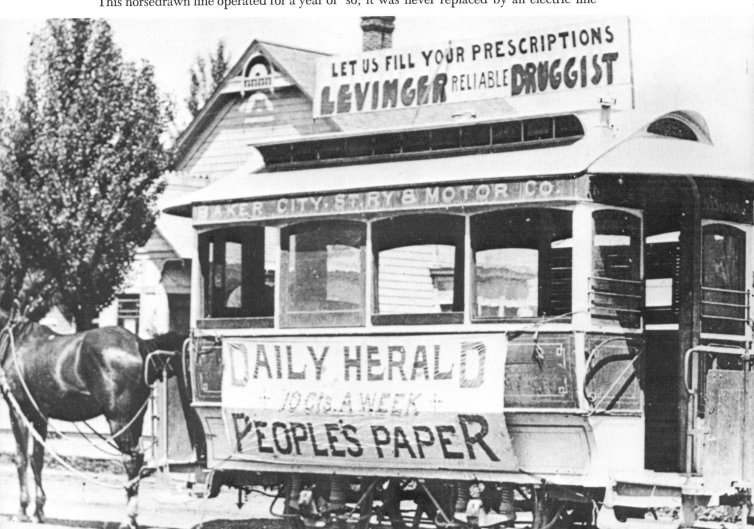

THE RED ELECTRICS (SP)

Southern Pacific was moving into the electrification field. Overhead wires were being strung along their tracks. Electric lines were the hit of the day. Some might have said that SP was following this program to keep up with the Oregon Electric. Others might have cited the rapidly growing suburban areas as SP's reason for moving into the field. One thing was clear: The Oregon country was growing and people needed transportation.

In 1914 the first of these electric cars were run from Portland through the upper western portion of the Willamette Valley. The Red Electric circle trip, as SP advertised it, was originally trackage of the old Oregon Central and the narrow gauge Oregonian Railway Company, Ltd., which was now a part of the SP system.

The SP painted their cars a smart red, and the public soon came to know them. The first of them had been purchased when the Portland Eugene & Eastern Railway Company had been acquired by SP.

The big Red Electrics began their run into the valley from Union Station in Portland, proceeding south on Fourth Street through the heart of the business district to what is today Barber Boulevard.

The Red Cars stopped frequently

The hot wire that supplies the juice to keep the Red Electric cars running

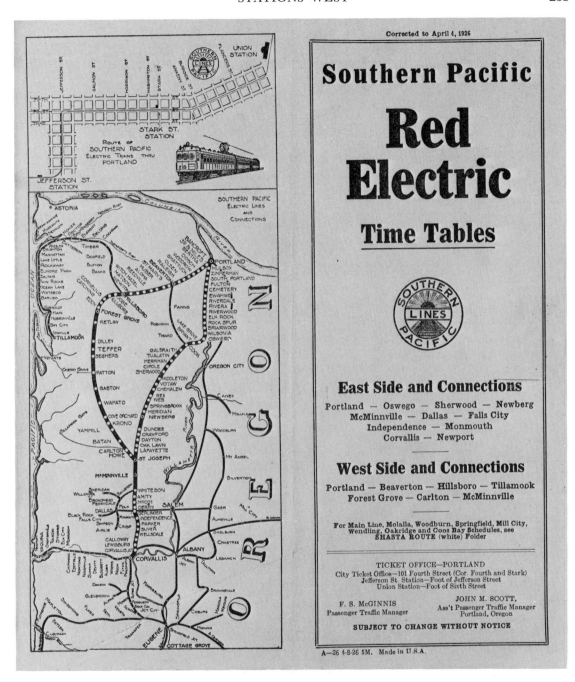

along Fourth Street to entrain passengers for valley points. It soon became evident an uptown ticket office was needed to accommodate these patrons. The first office was opened in 1917 at 131 Fourth Street, and in 1921 this was replaced by a larger ticket office only a block away, located at the corner of Fourth and Stark Streets.

Red Electric Trains
to and from
PORTLAND

TO PORTLAND—	†120	†134	*126	*124	*128	*130	*122	*140	*138	*136
Lv. McMinnville..	.....	.....	.....	7.45	.....	.....	3.17	.....	.....	.....
Carlton.......	.....	.....	.....	8.00	.....	.....	3.39	.....	.....	.....
Yamhill......	.....	.....	.....	8.06	.....	.....	3.45	.....	.....	.....
Forest Grove..	.....	†6.05	6.50	8.41	12.25	3.15	4.14	6.45	.....	.....
Hillsboro.....	.....	†6.20	7.05	9.04	12.46	3.29	4.29	6.58	.....	10.30
Beaverton....	†6.06	†6.45	7.29	9.26	1.06	3.55	4.52	7.22	8.59	10.48
Ar. Portland	†6.38	†7.25	8.15	10.10	1.45	4.40	5.35	8.00	9.30	11.20

FROM PORTLAND	*121	*127	*129	*123	†131	†133	*125	*137	*135	*139
Lv. Portland......	7.55	10.45	1.25	3.45	†4.45	†5.15	6.00	8.03	9.33	11.30
Beaverton.....	8.31	11.20	2.01	4.28	†5.19	†5.53	6.45	8.33	10.03	12.03
Hillsboro......	8.53	11.43	2.26	4.54	——	†6.18	7.10	——	10.25	12.25
Forest Grove...	9.16	11.59	2.40	5.15	.....	†6.35	7.25	.....	——	12.40
Yamhill.......	9.44	——	——	5.43	.....	——	.....	.....	.....	.....
Carlton........	9.55	.....	.....	5.51	.....	.....	.....	.....	.....	.....
Ar. McMinnville...	10.10	.....	.....	6.05	.....	.....	.....	.....	.....	.....

*Daily.   †Daily except Sundays.   Light face figures A.M, dark face P.M.

Buy Round-trip Tickets at Reduced Fares—
To Portland

From—	Week-End	15-Day	From—	Week-End	15-Day
Beaverton.........	$0.50	$0.60	Hillsboro..........	$0.85	$1.15
Carlton............	1.55	2.00	McMinnville.......	1.70	2.00
Forest Grove.......	1.10	1.50	Yamhill............	1.55	2.00

Week-end tickets on sale Fridays, Saturdays and Sundays; return limit Tuesday.   Fifteen-day tickets on sale daily; return limit 15 days; stopover privilege.

Please ask any Southern Pacific Agent for travel information.

 # Southern Pacific Lines

JOHN M. SCOTT,
Asst. Passenger Traffic Manager.

A-14 3-29-26 500

SOUTHERN PACIFIC IS PLEASED TO ANNOUNCE:

The opening our new $16,000 City Ticket Office, 131 Fourth Street in Portland, Saturday, January 27, 1917 from 8 P.M. to 10:30 P.M.

McElroy's Orchestra, one of Portland's best, playing two hours of fine music. Selections are:

1. March—"The American Spirit of Liberty" .... McElroy
2. Overture—"William Tell" .... Rossini
3. Waltz—"Spring, Beautiful Spring" .... Lincke
4. Trombone Solo—"The Evening Star" .... Wagner
    Mr. R. B. Powell
5. Selection from the Comic Opera "Mlle. Modiste" .... Herbert
6. (a) "Air de Ballet" .... Herbert
   (b) Idyl "The Glad Girl" .... Lampe
7. Medley—"Popular Airs" .... Lampe
8. Intermezzo—"Naila" .... Delibes
9. Grand American Fantasia .... Bendix
10. Finale—"Star Spangled Banner" ....

As an added attraction Southern Pacific has parked one of their new all steel-constructed electric trains in front of the City Ticket Office for public inspection. SP states:

> These trains are the only all steel-constructed electric trains operating out of Portland.

A further description of the City Ticket Office:

> The room is 40 feet wide and 100 feet long and is the largest room used by any transportation company in the Northwest for a ticket office.
> The main room is finished in cream and white with golden oak wainscoating and marble baseboards. The furniture in the room matches the woodwork and is of the best Eastern golden oak. The flooring is of white tile.

A description of the pictures on the walls of the new office:

> The frames are of golden oak. The size of the pictures are 40x80 inches and the frames are an additional 8 inches in width. The walls are paneled and the pictures occupy positions in the center of the panels. Some of the bromide enlargements of actual photographs: Crater Lake, Mount Shasta, Lake Tahoe, San Francisco Cliff House, Yosemite Valley, Orange Grove and a photo of the SP steamer that plies between New Orleans and New York with caption, "100 Golden Hours at Sea."
> The revolving folder rack at the front of the office contains 100 compartments and arrangements have been made for the rack to contain folders of all transportation companies of prominence in the U.S., Canada and Mexico.

A souvenir booklet from the opening of the Portland City Ticket Office in 1917

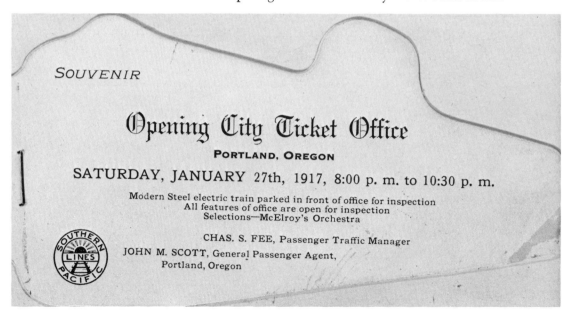

Portland City Ticket Office—131 Fourth Avenue. This office opened January 27, 1917

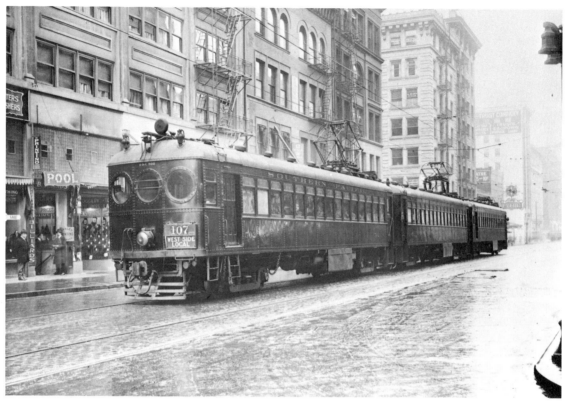

This 1920 photograph shows Red Electric SP train No. 107, the "West Side Local," ready to leave town, stops at the Fourth Street Ticket Office to entrain additional patrons.

Portland City Ticket Office—at the corner of Fourth and Stark. This office opened March 31, 1921

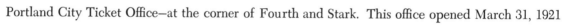

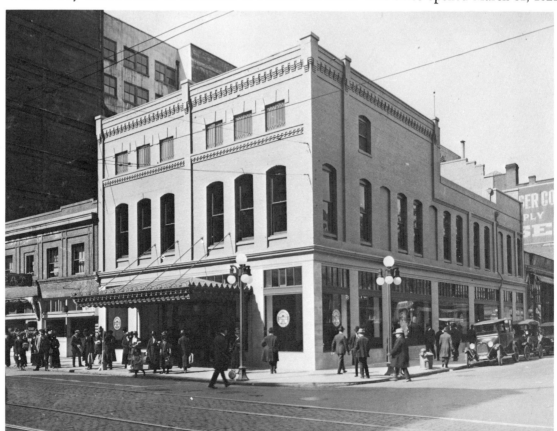

Electric Line Ticket Office

Parcel Room and Telephone Booths

This is a well equipped Ticket Office and waiting room with large comfortable ladies' rest room, parcel checking counter, public telephone booths, and all the conveniences which go to make a modern station.

Fifty-six electric trains use this station daily.

In these facilities we offer service. We invite you to demonstrate by your patronage the necessity for such conveniences.

CONVENIENCE and cheerfulness were the main ideas followed by Southern Pacific architects in remodeling this structure.

These thoughts are effectively carried out in the interior decoration; by the full windows on Fourth Street and on Stark Street; the light walls; the gray floor and rich golden, quartered oak woodwork. The results are distinctly pleasing.

So far electrical operation in Oregon has not been a financial success. Month by month the cost of operation is considerably more than the earnings.

The Southern Pacific needs your patronage, and in soliciting such patronage we take the liberty of inviting your attention to the fact that the Southern Pacific is a vital factor in the development of Western Oregon.

THE Southern Pacific operates an extensive electric system on the West Side of the Willamette River comprising the lines between Portland and Corvallis.

Southern Pacific red electric cars represent the "last word" in convenient, safe and rapid transportation.

We are putting forth every effort to make the operation of these electric lines a financial success.

Main Waiting Room

Ticket Counter

The inside of the brochure announcing the opening of the new Electric Line Ticket Office at the corner of Fourth and Stark Streets in Portland, 1921.

The "Oswego Local" Red Electric ready to leave Union Station. Engineer Bert Rohse is pictured here with his helpers. The conductor can be seen in the background examining his train orders.

The interior of a Red Electric car

Upper left, The Liberty Bell being pulled up Fourth Street in Portland by Red Electrics, July 15, 1915.

The Red Electric stopped at McMinnville enroute to Portland. This photo was taken about 1915

Bertha Station, like the track in front of it, has long ago been removed. This was one of the important stops on the Red Electrics. Today as one drives over the forked overpass of the Bertha-Beaverton highway, just west of Hillsdale and only a few miles out of Portland, one can see new homes and deluxe apartment complexes in all directions. Directly under the overpass was the former location of Bertha Station. This photograph was taken in 1913. The Oregon & California's manager, Richard Koehler, named the station after his wife. Bertha Station's only remembrance among railroad people is the disastrous head-on collision of two Electric trains causing heavy loss of life and injury in the early 20s.

Bertha Station May 9, 1920: This tragic head-on wreck of two Red Electric trains resulted in several deaths and many injuries at a well-known landmark in Portland. It happened beneath the overpass of the Beaverton Highway just west of Hillsdale. The photo was taken only an hour or so after impact. The window blind on top of the car covered the body of Engineer "Si" Willett.
Willett's body was held in this position for several hours before it could be freed.

This little town located on the Red Electrics was about an hour's run from Portland. This city was founded by the Quakers and is truly "a city of churches" with almost all major denominations represented. It is the home of former President Herbert Hoover. Agent George James with the Bowler can be seen in front of the station. This photo was taken in 1915.

Another stop on the Red Electric, 1920

In this 1920 photograph SP No. 357, the "East Side Local," "goes into the hole" to allow a train from the opposite direction to pass. The main line divides here with one track going to McMinn-ville while the other is a short cut back to Beaverton.

A steam train operating between Whiteson and Sheridan making a connection with the Red Elec-trics at Whitson during World War I.

Conductor Walter Kimmell (extreme left) and his crew pose for the camera while waiting for a connecting train at Whiteson.

Elk Rock trestle, built in 1888, and Riverdale Station can be seen in this photograph. The Red Electric cars slowed down to 10 mph as they crossed the trestle. Frequently, rolling rocks and gravel, jarred free by the movement of the train would fall on the roof of the passing cars and some of the passengers would become very frightened.

In 1921 SP opened the Elk Rock tunnel eliminating both the station and the trestle. In the background the smokestack of the old Oswego Iron Company can be seen. This company had as its goal the making of the city of Oswego into the "Pittsburg of the West."

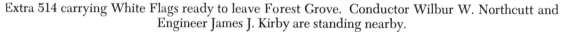

Extra 514 carrying White Flags ready to leave Forest Grove. Conductor Wilbur W. Northcutt and Engineer James J. Kirby are standing nearby.

The end of the line for the Red Electrics. Note the steam train bound for Corvallis passing on the opposite side from the station.

Freight motor PEE-100 along the line repairing the Red Electric's overhead wires

This short electric line was built from West Linn to the Tualatin River in 1893. It supplied the paper mill at Oregon City with some one-hundred cords of wood each day in order to keep their plant in operation. The line went through several ownerships. A very elaborate station was constructed at West Linn and a white colored street car was operated from the Tualatin River through the cities of Willamette, West Linn and to a short distance beyond Bolton.

TO Magones from Tualatin River, Willamette, Junction, West Linn and Bolton — SOUTHERN PACIFIC

STATIONS	*2	*4	*6	*8	*10	*12	*14	*16	*18	*20	*22	*24	*26	*28	*30
Lv. Tualatin River	.....	6.23	6.54	.....	7.24	.....	8.03	.....	8.36	.....	10.38	11.33	.....	12.56	1.48
Willamette	.....	6.25	6.56	.....	7.26	.....	8.05	.....	f 8.38	9.45	10.40	11.35	12.25	f12.58	1.50
Junction	.....	f 6.37	f 7.07	.....	f 7.37	.....	f 8.17	.....	f 8.50	f 9.57	f10.52	f11.47	f12.37	f 1.08	f 2.02
Ar. West Linn	.....	6.39	7.09	.....	7.39	.....	8.19	.....	8.53	10.00	10.55	11.50	12.39	1.10	2.05
Lv. West Linn	6.20	.....	.....	6.55	.....	7.35	.....	8.20	9.15	10.00	10.55	11.50	.....	1.10	2.05
Bolton	f	.....	.....	f	.....	f	.....	f	f	f	f	.....	f	f	
Ar. Magones	6.27	.....	.....	7.02	.....	7.42	.....	8.27	9.22	10.07	11.02	11.57	.....	1.17	2.12

STATIONS	*32	*34	*36	*40	*42	*44	*46	*48	*50	*52	*54	*56	*58	*60	*62
Lv. Tualatin River	.....	3.20	4.31	5.31	.....	.....	.....	6.30	7.01	7.46	8.31	9.26	10.26	11.26	12.41
Willamette	2.35	3.22	f 4.33	f 5.32	.....	6.00	.....	6.32	7.03	7.48	8.33	9.28	10.28	11.28	f12.42
Junction	f 2.47	f 3.34	f 4.45	f 5.41	.....	f 6.12	.....	f 6.42	f 7.12	f 7.57	f 8.42	f 9.37	f10.37	11.37	12.50
Ar. West Linn	2.50	3.37	4.48	5.44	.....	6.14	.....	6.44	7.15	8.00	8.45	9.40	10.40	11.40	12.53
Lv. West Linn	2.50	3.37	5.00	.....	5.45	.....	6.15	.....	7.15	8.00	8.45	9.45	10.45	12.15	.....
Bolton	f	f	f	.....	f	.....	f	.....	f	f	f	f	f	12.20	.....
Ar. Magones	2.57	3.44	5.07	.....	5.52	.....	6.22	.....	7.22	8.07	8.52	9.52	10.52	.....	.....

Light face A. M., Dark face P. M. Subject to change without notice. f Flag. * Daily. Corrected to May 10, 1925.
Pub. No. A-22. 5-25-25. 1M.

FROM Magones to Bolton, West Linn, Junction, Willamette and Tualatin River — SOUTHERN PACIFIC

STATIONS	*1	*3	*5	*7	*9	*11	*13	*15	*17	*19	*21	*23	*25	*27	*29
Lv. Magones	.....	.....	6.28	.....	7.03	.....	7.43	.....	8.28	9.23	10.08	11.03	11.58	.....	1.18
Bolton	.....	.....	f	.....	f	.....	f	.....	f	f	f	f	f	.....	f
Ar. West Linn	.....	.....	6.35	.....	7.10	.....	7.50	.....	8.35	9.30	10.15	11.10	12.05	.....	1.25
Lv. West Linn	6.05	6.40	.....	7.10	.....	7.40	.....	8.20	.....	9.30	10.15	11.10	12.10	12.40	1.25
Junction	f 6.08	f 6.42	.....	f 7.12	.....	f 7.43	.....	f 8.23	.....	f 9.33	f10.18	f11.13	f12.13	f12.43	f 1.28
Willamette	6.20	6.51	.....	7.21	.....	7.55	.....	8.33	.....	9.44	10.30	11.25	12.24	12.53	1.40
Ar. Tualatin River	6.22	6.53	.....	7.23	.....	7.59	.....	8.35	.....	.....	10.34	11.29	.....	12.55	1.44

STATIONS	*31	*33	*35	*39	*41	*43	*45	*47	*49	*51	*53	*55	*57	*59	*61
Lv. Magones	2.13	2.58	3.45	5.08	.....	5.53	.....	6.23	.....	7.23	8.08	8.53	9.53	10.53	.....
Bolton	f	f	f	f	.....	f	.....	f	.....	f	f	f	f	f	12.21
Ar. West Linn	2.20	3.05	3.52	5.15	.....	6.00	.....	6.30	.....	7.30	8.15	9.00	10.00	11.00	12.25
Lv. West Linn	2.20	3.05	4.15	5.15	5.45	.....	6.15	.....	6.45	7.30	8.15	9.10	10.10	11.10	12.25
Junction	f 2.23	f 3.07	f 4.18	f 5.18	f 5.48	.....	f 6.17	.....	f 6.48	f 7.33	f 8.18	f 9.13	f10.13	11.13	f12.28
Willamette	2.34	3.17	4.28	f 5.28	5.59	.....	6.27	.....	6.58	7.43	8.28	9.23	10.23	11.23	f12.38
Ar. Tualatin River	.....	3.19	4.30	5.35	.....	.....	6.29	.....	7.00	7.45	8.30	9.25	10.25	11.25	12.40

Light face A. M., Dark face P. M. Subject to change without notice. f Flag. * Daily. Corrected to May 10, 1925.

A timetable for the year 1925. By this time the line was under the ownership of the Southern Pacific.

CHAPTER 29

This was a short fifteen mile line extending into southern Washington. It was found to be too expensive and impractical to continue building the line from Vancouver to Yakima so the name "Yakima" was changed to "Yacolt." This photograph shows the first train ferrying from Portland to Vancouver, Washington, across the Columbia River in April, 1903. Portland, Vancouver & Yakima Railroad Co.

A short line railroad built from Milton Creek on Scappoose Bay along the Columbia River south to the Nehalem Valley, penetrating one of the finest forest regions of the coastal area. Passenger service was used here to reach some of these remote areas. This photograph was taken about 1915.

A twenty-seven mile line built shortly after the turn of the century from Thrall, California, to Pokegama, Oregon, with only about seven miles of track in the state of Oregon. Its sole existence was based on the handling of forest products, particularly logs. This photo was taken about 1905. It shows a train crossing the Klamath River. The name on the equipment, Oregon Southern, was a former name for the line. Yakima Lake Railroad Company.

On account of the Election on Saturday, Nov.
27, 1909, to make Siskiyou County DRY,
The Klamath Lake Railroad will run a

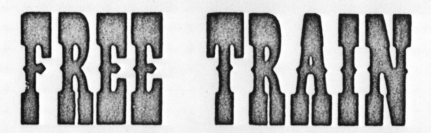

FREE TRAIN

On that day to accommodate
such voters as can conven=
iently use it.

The train will leave Pokegama at 8 A. M., and returning
will leave Thrall at 2:45 P. M., after arrival of No. 15, S. P.,
if that train is on time. This train both going and coming
will stop on Signal to take on or let off Passengers at nearest point to their homes.

E. T. ABBOTT, General Manager.

Remember NO FARES WILL
BE COLLECTED

Handbill from the collection
of the Klamath County Museum

Klamath Lake Railroad
~~McIntyre Steam Stage Line~~

1 Tues. Thurs. Sat.	Miles	STATIONS	Elev'n.	2 Tues. Thurs. Sat.
6.30	0.0	Lv..................THRALL..................Ar.	2138	1.15
6.59	5.8	..................Bogus..................	2192	12.47
7.19	9.8	..................Steel Bridge..................	2270	12.28
7.30	12.0	..................Fall Creek..................	2578	12.17
7.37	13.3	..................Klamath Springs..................	2795	12.10
7.50	15.0	..................Top Switch Back..................	3018	11.58
8.00	17.1	..................Ways..................	3320	11.48
8.20	21.3	..................Dixie..................	3752	11.29
8.35	24.3	Ar..................POKEGAMA..................Lv.	3720	11.15
8.50	0.0	Lv. (Stage)........Pokegama..................Ar.	....	11.00
4.00	34.0	Ar..................KLAMATH FALLS..................Lv.	....	4.00

Trains connect at Klamath Springs with Stage for Beswick, Hot Springs Hotel and Picard.

A representative of the Klamath Lake Railroad Company will be at Thrall station upon arrival of all Southern Pacific trains and assist passengers to hotel without charge.

This small ten mile line was built in 1937 from Gilchrist Junction on the Southern Pacific to the town of Gilchrist. The latter is a lumber town owned and controlled by the Gilchrist Timber people.

CARLTON & COAST RAILROAD COMPANY.

J. C. FLORA, President.   Carlton, Ore.

ED. KINGSLEY, First Vice-President.   Portland, Ore.

GEO. L. GARDNER, Second Vice-President,   ,,

THOS. RICHARDSON, Secretary,   Carlton, Ore.

	25 Motor.	Mls	*February*, 1931.		22 Motor.		
....	....	....	LEAVE]	[ARRIVE	....	....	......
....	†11 30 A M	0	........**Carlton**.......		9 00 A M	....	......
....	11 33 ,,	1	........Johnson.........		8 56 ,,	....	......
....	11 53 A M	5.2	.........Woods..........		8 36 ,,	....	......
....	12 01 P M	7.3	..........Pike...........		8 28 ,,	....	......
....	12 15 ,,	10.7	......Cedar Creek......		8 15 ,,	....	......
....	12 20 ,,	12.0	......Fairchilds.......		8 10 ,,	....	......
....	12 22 ,,	12.1	.....Chesterbrook		8 08 ,,	....	......
....	12 30 P M	14.1	... **Tillamook Gate** ...		†8 00 A M	....	......
....	....	....	ARRIVE]	[LEAVE	....	....	......

Trains marked † run daily except Sunday.

STANDARD—*Pacific time.*

Connection.—At Carlton—With Southern Pacific Co.

This line was built in 1910 from Carlton, a station on the Southern Pacific near McMinnville. It was intended to reach the city of Tillamook but lack of finances prevented it from reaching this destination. The line was built some thirteen miles to a point known as Tillamook Gate only a short distance from the Coast Range Mountains. It was a logging line operating as a public carrier. This 1910 photo taken at Carlton shows some of the rolling stock including passenger equipment.

This five and a half mile line was built in 1912 from Patton, on the Southern Pacifiic near Gaston, to the town of Cherry Grove. The line was built to serve the surrounding agricultural areas as well as the timber interests. It was soon found that the promoters of Cherry Grove should have named their town Walnut Grove—as cherries did very poorly while walnuts did very well. This photograph was taken in Cherry Grove about 1915. The station is visible in the background.

CHAPTER 30

The only operating trolley museum in the Northwest is located at Glenwood, Oregon. The Oregon Electric Historical Society has acquired street cars from all over the world. The open air car shown here is from Australia.

This is the upper terminus of the PORTLAND ZOO RAILWAY. This thirty inch gauge railway has several miles of trackage running through the Portland Zoological Gardens. This small railroad enjoys the patronage of thousands of Portland visitors annually.

Jetties are built to protect the channels for large estuaries flowing into the Pacific Ocean. They are built on pilings with a small road bed permitting narrow gauge rail operation. Large boulders are dropped into the foaming ocean to prevent sands from shifting into the passageway. This photograph shows the jetty at Barview in Tillamook County, 1910.

This photograph of a jetty at Astoria was taken about 1900

In this 1894 photo the Newport jetty is shown with a steam locomotive and several narrow gauge cars carrying rock.

Russian Decapods (2-10-0 coal burners) being shipped from Portland to Russia during World War II. These locomotives were built by the Baldwin Locomotive Works under the lend-lease program.

Left and above: Locomotives for Russia, World War II

INDEX

— A —

Airlie Branch, 163
Airlie, Oregon, 69, 158, 159
Akin, Carl F., 156
Albany & Lebanon Railroad Co., 133
Albany, Oregon, 27, 28, 82, 85, 133, 148, 201, 203, 210, 211, 214, 222, 226, 227
Allen, Wm., 116
Alpine, Oregon, 148
Alsea, Oregon, 148
Alvadore, Oregon, 149
American Legion, 211
Anderson, Oregon, 185
Arbor Lodge, Oregon, 178
Ashland, Oregon, 13, 37, 38, 142
Astor Expedition, 21
Astoria & Columbia River Railroad Co., 106, 107, 115, 116, 117, 118, 119, 121
Astoria, Oregon, 82, 115, 116, 117, 118, 119, 121, 122, 224, 225, 256
Astoria-Seaside Line, 115, 117, 118, 119, 121
Astoria & South Coast Railway Co., 115, 118
Athena, Oregon, 63
Aumsville, Oregon, 72
Aurora, Oregon, 19
Austin, Oregon, 91

— B —

Baker Bridge, Oregon, 150
Baker, Oregon, V, 59, 91, 92, 93, 95, 229
Baldwin Locomotive Works, 257
Barber Boulevard, 230
Barton, Jack, 173
Barton, Oregon, 185
Barview, Oregon, 113, 256
Bates, Oregon, 95
Bay City, Oregon, 114
Bay Ocean, Oregon, 114
Beaver Creek, Oregon, 197
Beaver Hill Mine, 136
Beaver Spur, Oregon, 218
Beaverton, Oregon, 7, 108, 134, 135, 210, 232, 242
Beaverton & Willsburg Railroad Co., 134, 135
Bellevue, Oregon, 65
Bend, Oregon, 123, 124, 125, 126, 128, 129, 130, 161, 162

Bennett, Si, 80
Benton County, 82
Bertha-Beaverton Highway, 240
Bertha, Oregon, 240
Bewley, John, 160
Bieber, California, 130
Bieber Route, 130
Big Creek & Telocaset RR, 96
Biggs, Oregon, 100, 101
Bilbrey, James M., 200
Bill of Lading, 25
Bingham Springs, Oregon, 55
Black Butte, California, 142, 145
Black Rock, Oregon, 163, 165, 167, 168
Bly, Oregon, 161, 162
Bohemia Gold Mines, 151
Bolton, Oregon, 246, 247
Bonneville, Oregon, 50
Bonney, Paul K., 28
Boring, Oregon, 185, 192
Bourne, Oregon, 91
Breakwater Steamer, 137
Bridal Veil, Oregon, 56
Broadacres, Oregon, 206
Broadmead, Oregon, 156
Brogan, Oregon, 96
Brooklyn Shops, 15, 134
Brownsville, Oregon, 20, 65, 77, 133, 144
Buick, Richard, 30
Bullrun, Oregon, 190, 191
Burlington Northern Railroad, 63, 115, 161
Burlington, Oregon, 202, 217
Burns, Oregon, 91, 99
Butler, N. L. "Tack", 80
Butte Falls, Oregon, 132

— C —

Calapooyo Mountains, 151
California Express, 38
California & Northeastern Railroad, 142
California & Oregon Coast Railroad Co., 143, 147
Call Building, 86
Camp One, Oregon, 122
Canby, Oregon, 18
Canemah Park, 184, 187, 188, 191
Canyon City, Oregon, 91
Carlton & Coast Railroad Co., 252
Carlton, Oregon, 232, 241, 252
Carver, Oregon, 150

Carver, Stephen, 96, 148, 150
Cascade Line, 96, 142, 144, 145
Cascade Portage Railroad, 43
Cascades, 11, 43
Casteel, Arthur, 85, 88
Casteel, Dick, 90
Cazadero, Oregon, 184, 185, 186, 188, 189, 190, 191, 193
Cedarville Park, 191
Celilo, Oregon, 44
Central, Oregon, 100, 123, 125, 128, 130
Central Pacific Railroad, 44
Central Railway of Oregon, 60
Chautauqua Station, 16, 183
Chemult, Oregon, 129, 130
Cherry Grove, Oregon, 253
Cheyenne, Wyoming, 9
Chicago, Illinois, 47, 63, 77, 104, 120
Chicago & Northwestern Railway Co., 104
City of Prineville Railroad, 128, 129
City & Suburban Railway Co., 16, 178
Clackamas County, 11, 150, 182
Clackamas County National Guard, 183, 195
Clackamas, Oregon, 15, 134
Clackamas River, 150
Clark, Bob, 80
Clatsop Beach, 117, 121
Clatsop County, 118
Cliff House, 233
Cloverdale, Oregon, 179
Coast Range, 106, 108, 252
Coburg, Oregon, 3, 4, 65, 70, 75
Cochran, Oregon, 108
Columbia City, Oregon, 7
Columbia & Nehalem River Railroad, 249
Columbia River, 43, 44, 48, 55, 57, 64, 82, 98, 100, 115, 117, 119, 122, 128, 129, 179, 248, 249
Columbia River & Blue Mountain Railroad Co., 57
Columbia River Gorge, 48
Columbia Southern Railway, 100, 101, 102
Condit, Addie, 72
Condit, Henry Beecher, 74, 75
Condit, Ross, 72

Condon, Kinzua & Southern Railroad Co., 97
Condon, Oregon, 97
Cook, Oregon, 134, 135, 242
Coos Bay & Eastern Railroad Co., 136
Coos Bay Lines, 137, 139, 141
Coos Bay, Oregon, (Marshfield), 135, 137, 138
Coos Bay, Roseburg & Eastern Railroad & Navigation Co. 136, 137
Copenhaver, M.D., 14
Coquille, Oregon, 139
Corvallis & Alsea River Railway Company, 148
Corvallis & Eastern Railroad Co., 83, 84, 85, 88
Corvallis, Oregon, 28, 39, 40, 78, 82, 83, 85, 88, 148, 228, 231, 237, 245
Cottage Grove, Oregon, 151, 152, 155
Couch Lake, Portland, 7
Cove, Oregon, 60
Crane, Oregon, 161, 162
Crater Lake, 233
Creswell, Oregon, 31
Crystal Lake Park, 191
Culp's Creek, Oregon, 151
Culp, Edward A., V, 57
Culp, John, 151
Currinsville, Oregon, 185

– D –
Daddy Train, 118
Dairy, Oregon, 161
Dallas & Deschutes Railroad Co., 43
Dallas, Oregon, 4, 65, 80, 81, 158, 159, 163, 165, 166, 167
Daly, Fred, 76
Davenport, Homer Calvin, 73, 74
Dayton, Oregon, 65, 78, 223
Dayton, Sheridan & Grand Ronde Railroad Co., 65, 66, 78
De Autremont Bros., 34
Dee, Oregon, 105
Deschutes Canyon, 100, 123
Deschutes Railroad, 123, 125, 127
Deschutes River, 124
Detroit Dam, 85, 90
Detroit, Michigan, 196
Detroit, Oregon, 90
Dimick, Grant, 195
Disston, Oregon, 151, 152
Doodle Bug, 169
Down, James, 71
Down's, Oregon, 71
Duff, 73, 74
Dufur, Oregon, 103
Dummy, The, 179
Dundee, Oregon, 4, 5, 65, 69

– E –
Eagle Creek, Oregon, 185
Eagle Point, Oregon, 132
Earhart, R. P., 46
Earl of Airlie, 65
East Independence, Oregon, 211
East Morrison Street Station, 14
East Portland, Oregon, 9, 11, 75, 134, 179
East Side Line, 13, 28
"East Side Local," 242
East Side Railway Co., 182, 183
Eccles, David C., 91
Echo, Oregon, 52
Elgin, Oregon, 60
Elk City, Oregon, 85
Elkrock Trestle, 243
Elk Rock Tunnel, 244
Enterprise, Oregon, 61
Eola, Oregon, 165
Estacada, Oregon, 184, 185, 186, 188, 189, 190, 191
Eugene, Oregon, 13, 28, 29, 96, 136, 137, 138, 140, 141, 142, 144, 145, 148, 199, 200, 201, 203, 206, 212, 213, 214, 215, 222, 228
Evergreen, Oregon, 194

– F –
Fairview, Oregon, 48
Falls City, Oregon, 163, 165
Fillmore, Oregon, 71
Flavel, Oregon, 119, 120
Forest Grove, Oregon, 201, 205, 206, 224, 231, 232, 244
Fort Vancouver, Washington, 207
Foulds, J. M., 206
Fourth Street, 79, 134, 230, 231, 233, 234, 235, 236, 237, 239
French Prairie, Oregon, 21, 207
Friend, Oregon, 103
Fulquartz Landing, 4, 65
Fulton Park, Oregon, 78, 79

– G –
Gales Creek & Wilson River Railroad, 221
Garden Home, Oregon, 205
Gardiner, Oregon, 137
Garibaldi, Oregon, 111
Gaston, Oregon, 253
Gault, Mr., 183
Gearhart, Oregon, 120
Geer, Theodore Thurston, 6
Geiser, Oregon, 91
General, The, 154, 155
Gerlinger, Fritz, 163
Gerlinger, Louis, 163, 165
Gerlinger, Oregon, 166, 167, 168
German-Catholic Settlement, 71
Gervais, Oregon, 21
Gibbon, Oregon, 55
Gilchrist, Oregon, 251

Gilchrist Timber Co., 251
Gilliam County, 97
Gladstone, Oregon, 183
Gladstone Park, 16
Glenbrook, Oregon, 148
Glendale, Oregon, 31
Glenwood, Oregon, 221, 254
Goble, Oregon, 7, 64, 115, 118
Golf Junction, Oregon, 186
Gramse, Mrs., 59
Grande Ronde Valley, 57, 60
Granger, Wyoming, 104
Grants Pass, Oregon, 35, 147
Great Northern Railway, 106, 161
Great Northern Steamship, 119, 120, 123, 129, 130, 131
Great Southern Railroad, 103
Gresham, Oregon, 185, 191, 194
Griffitts, Dick, 177

– H –
Hagey, Andrew, 76
Halley, Joe, 200
Hallsferry, Oregon, 209
Hammond, Andrew Benoni, 83, 85, 117, 118
Hammond, Oregon, 121
Harbor Drive, 79
Harney County, 99
Harriman, Edward H., IX, 96, 100, 106, 123, 124, 128, 225
Harris, C. Keith, 25
Harrison, Benjamin, 17
Harrisburg, Oregon, 209
Hawthorne Avenue, 150
Hawthorne Bridge, 79, 199
Hayden Island, 179
Hayden Landing, Oregon, 179, 180
Heimrich, John, 103
Henning, Marion David, 21
Heppner Branch, 62
Heppner Junction, 62
Heppner, Oregon, 62
Hermiston, Oregon, 52
Hill, James J., IX, 106, 109, 123, 124, 128, 129, 131, 132, 216
Hillsboro, Oregon, 7, 13, 28, 106, 107, 108, 115, 118, 134, 232
Hillsdale, Oregon, 240
Hilton, Walter E., 40
Edward Hines Lumber Co., 99
Hinshaw, Harold A., 25
Hoag, Wm. M., 82
Hoeflein, Wm. C., 85
Hogg, Thomas Egerton, 82, 84, 85
Hoggs' Pass, 84
Holladay, Ben, 11, 12, 13, 19, 22, 32, 39, 43, 75
Holladay, Oregon, 116
Hood River, Oregon, 50, 51, 105
Hoover, Herbert C., 22, 24, 241
Hoskins, Oregon, (Fort Hoskins), 172, 175
Hot Lake, Oregon, 53, 57

Hubbard, Oregon, 21
Hudson's Bay Co., 207
Hunt, George W., 63
Huntington, Oregon, 44, 47, 59, 104
Hunt Party, 21
Hunt Railroad, 63

— I —
Ilwaco Railway & Steam Navigation Co., 98
Ilwaco, Washington, 98
Independence & Monmouth Railway Company, 158, 159
Independence, Oregon, 39, 40, 158, 159, 160, 172, 173, 174, 176, 177
Indian Valley, 60
Interstate Bridge, 64, 179
Ione, Oregon, 62
Irvine, V. L., 42
Irwin, Mollie, 92

— J —
Jacksonville, Oregon, 169, 170, 171
Jacobs, Sidney, 10
James, George, 241
Jefferson, Oregon, 26
Jefferson Street Terminal, 79, 80, 134, 199, 200, 203
Jennings Lodge, Oregon, 192
Jester, G. P., 36
Junction City, Oregon, 28, 39
Jetty Railroads—Astoria 256, Barview 256, Newport 257
John Day, Oregon, 91
Johnson's Landing, Oregon, 122
Johnstone, William B., 108
Jones, Jack, 10
Joseph (Town), 60
Joseph Branch, 60
Joseph, Chief, 60
Juntura, Oregon, 100

— K —
Kalama, Washington, 7, 64, 115
Kansas Central, 178
Keasey, Oregon, 216
Keaton, Buster, 154, 155
Keil, Wilhelm, Dr., 19
Kelley, Orrin, 81
Kimes, Vale, 134
Kimmell, Walter, 243
Kinzua, Oregon, 97
Kirby, James J., 27, 244
Kirk, Oregon, 144
Klamath Falls Municipal Railway, 160, 161
Klamath Falls, Oregon, 129, 130, 142, 143, 144, 161, 162, 229, 251
Klamath Lake Railroad Co., 249, 250, 251
Klamath Northern Railway, 251
Klamath River, 249
Koehler, Richard, 240

— L —
La Grande, Oregon, 57, 58, 60
Lake Lytle Hotel, 110
Lake Lytle, Oregon, 110
Lake Pend Oreille, Idaho, 44
Lake Tahoe, 233
Lakeview, Oregon, 146, 161, 162
Land Grant Act (U.S. Federal), 11, 65
Larson, Carl E., 25
Laseiur, Geo., 200
Lasen, Oregon, 212
Lebanon Junction, Oregon, 133
Lebanon, Oregon, 133, 134
Lend-Lease Program, 257, 258, 259
Lewis & Clark Exposition, 186
Liberty Bell, 239
Limited Mail, 50
Linkville, Oregon (Klamath Falls), 229
Linkville Trolley, 229
Linneman Junction, Oregon, 193
Linnton, Oregon, 202, 216
Livesley, Oregon, 208
Lockner, Joseph, 10
Longview, Portland & Northern Railway, 154, 158
Lytle, Elmer Elm, 100, 106, 110

— M —
McCormick, Ralph C., 25
McElroy's Orchestra, 233, 234
McKeen, Motor, 31, 164, 168
McKeen, Wm. R., 168
McLoughlin, Dr. John, 207
McMinnville, Oregon, 13, 39, 42, 78, 232, 239, 242, 252
Macleay, Oregon, 3, 4, 5, 6
Magones, Oregon, 247
Madras, Oregon, 127
Malheur Canyon, 96
Malheur Junction, Oregon, 96
Malheur Valley Railway Co., 96
Mapleton, Oregon, 138, 141
Margey, 4
Marion County, 6, 84, 195
Marion, Oregon, 26
Markee, Archie S., 18
Marshfield, Oregon (Coos Bay), 136, 137, 138
Marshville, Oregon, 15
Mathews, Milo C., 200
Maupin, Oregon, 126, 127
Meadow View, Oregon, 213
Medford & Crater Lake Railroad, 132
Medford, Oregon, 37, 132, 169, 170, 171
Megler, Washington, 98
Methodist Missionaries, 208
Miller, Henry, 100
Merlin, Oregon, 35
Messal, Harlan H., 15

Mill City, Oregon, 90
Miller, James L., 10
Miller, Joaquin, 37
Milton Creek, 249
Milton, Oregon, 56, 220
Milwaukie, Oregon, 191
Minneapolis, Minnesota, 63
Minthorn, Henry J., Dr., 22
Modoc Indians, 18
Mohler, Oregon, 107
Molalla, Oregon, 195
Monmouth, Oregon, 158, 159
Monroe, Oregon, 148, 149
Montavilla, Oregon, 190, 191
Montgomery, R. K., 31, 36, 40
Moon, Dad, 97
Moores, Pres. I. R., 11
Morris, G. C., 37
Morrison, Oregon, 86
Morrow County, 62
Mosier, Oregon, 52
Mt. Angel, Oregon, 20, 71, 72, 185, 195, 196, 197, 198
Mount Hood Hotel, 50
Mount Hood, Oregon, 48, 105
Mount Hood, Railroad Co., 50, 105
Mount Shasta, 233
Mudgett, Harry D., 10
Multnomah County, 11, 182
Multnomah Falls, Oregon, 48, 49
Munra, Katherine Sterrett, 51
Myrtle Point, Oregon, 136, 139

— N —
Nahcotta, Washington, 98
Narrow Gauge Railroads, 3, 20, 43, 44, 65, 67, 69, 70, 71, 73, 75, 77, 78, 79, 133, 134, 146, 159, 230, 256, 257
Natron Cut-Off, 129, 144, 145
Necanicum Inn, 118
Necanicum River, 118
Nehalem Valley, 249
Nevada - California - Oregon Railroad, 91, 146, 147, 161
Newberg, Oregon, 69, 134, 241
New Era, Oregon, 18
Newbury, John C., 18
New Orleans, La., 233
Newport, Oregon, 84, 86, 88, 257
New York, New York, 77, 233
Nez Perce Indians, 60
Niagara, Oregon, 89
North Albina, Oregon, 178
North Bank Trains, 119
North Bend, Oregon, 137, 138, 140
North Coast Gasoline Motors, 58
Northcutt, Wilbur W., 244
Northern Pacific Railway Co., 7, 44, 47, 63, 64, 115, 118, 120, 220
Northern Pacific Steamship, 119
Northern Pacific Terminal Co., 9, 10

North Plains, Oregon, 202, 219
Noti, Oregon, 141

— O —
Oakland, Oregon, 13
Oakridge, Oregon, 142, 144
Oaks, The, 184, 186
Occidental Hotel, 228
Ockley Green, Oregon, 178
Ogden, Utah, 9
Old Betsy, 75, 76
Olsen, Stanley, 167
Omaha, Nebraska, 9
One Hundred Golden Hours at Sea, 233
Oneonta, II
Ontario, Oregon, 104
Oregon & California Ferry, 9, 13
Oregon and California Railroad Co., 6, 7, 11, 12, 13, 15, 18, 19, 20, 22, 25, 28, 29, 32, 36, 37, 39, 43, 44, 65, 69, 75, 78, 133, 134, 169, 240
Oregon & Northwestern Railroad, 99
Oregon & Southeastern Railroad, 151, 152, 153, 155
Oregon & Washington Territory Railroad, 63
Oregon, California & Eastern Railway, 160, 161, 162
Oregon Central Railroad Co., 11, 39, 134, 238
Oregon City, Oregon, 7, 16, 17, 28, 43, 134, 182, 183, 185, 186, 187, 188, 190, 195, 196, 246
Oregon Coast, 106
Oregon Electric Historical Society, 254
Oregon Electric Railway Co., IX, 20, 199, 200, 201, 202, 203, 204, 205, 206, 207, 208, 209, 210, 211, 212, 213, 214, 215, 230
Oregon Land Company, 22
Oregonian Railway Co., Ltd., 4, 20, 44, 65, 66, 67, 68, 69, 70, 71, 73, 75, 77, 78, 79, 80, 133, 134, 159, 230
Oregon Pacific & Eastern Railway, 151, 153
Oregon Pacific Railroad, 82, 83, 84, 85, 87
Oregon Railway & Navigation Co., II, V, 7, 43, 44, 45, 46, 47, 48, 50, 51, 55, 57, 59, 60, 62, 96, 97, 98, 100, 103, 104
Oregon Short Line, 44, 47, 59, 96, 104
Oregon Southern Railroad, 249
Oregon Steam Navigation Co., 43
Oregon Steamship Co., 43
Oregon Territory, 17
Oregon Trunk Railway, 123, 124, 125, 127, 128, 129, 130, 161

Oregon-Washington Railroad & Navigation Co., 125
Oregon Water Power & Railway Co., 182, 184, 185, 186
Oriental Limited, 131
Oro Dell, Oregon, 57
Oswego Iron Co., 244
"Oswego Local," 237
Oswego, Oregon, 69, 79, 134, 135, 244
OWL Train, 214

— P —
Pacific Coast, 114, 148
Pacific & Eastern Railway, 132
Pacific Hotel, 59
Pacific Northwest, 120, 131, 163, 195
Pacific Ocean, 82, 84, 112, 117, 118, 256
Pacific Railway & Navigation Co., 106, 107, 108, 110, 111, 113
Panama Canal, 120
Panama-Pacific Exposition, 120
Parkdale, Oregon, 105
Parker House, 116, 119
Parrot Creek, Oregon, 11, 75
Patton, Edwin Cooke, IX
Patton, Oregon, 253
Patton Post Card Company, IX
Pendleton, Oregon, 54, 63
Peninsula, Oregon, 178
Perrydale, Oregon, 65
Philomath College, 86
Philomath, Oregon, 83, 86
Piedmont, Oregon, 179
Pioneer, Oregon, 86
Pittsburg of the West, 244
Pilot Rock Junction, Oregon, 97
Polk County, 163
Pokegama, Oregon, 249, 250, 251
Ponderosa Pine, 96
Pondosa, Oregon, 96
Portage Railroad, II, 43
Portland & Coos Bay Steamship Line, 137
Portland & Oregon City Railway Company, 150
Portland & Southwestern Railroad, 122
Portland & Vancouver Railway, 179, 181
Portland & Willamette Valley Railway Co., 4, 69, 79, 80, 134
Portland, Astoria & Pacific Railway Co., 216, 218
Portland Electric Power Co., 182, 193, 194
Portland, Eugene & Eastern Railway Company, 148, 222, 223, 225, 227, 230, 246
Portland, Oregon, 3, 4, 5, 7, 11, 13, 14, 16, 17, 20, 23, 28, 29, 37, 39, 43, 44, 47, 48, 50, 65, 69, 73, 78,

79, 81, 82, 98, 104, 106, 108, 109, 111, 112, 115, 116, 117, 118, 119, 120, 122, 124, 125, 134, 136, 137, 145, 148, 150, 156, 166, 178, 179, 182, 185, 186, 189, 190, 191, 193, 196, 199, 200, 201, 202, 203, 205, 206, 208, 210, 211, 212, 214, 215, 216, 217, 218, 222, 223, 225, 230, 231, 232, 233, 234, 235, 236, 237, 239, 240, 241, 248, 255, 257
Portland Oregonian, 3, 5, 6, 123
Portland Railroad Yards, 7
Portland Railway Light & Power Co., 182, 185, 187, 188, 189, 190, 191, 192, 195
Portland Terminal Railroad Co., 10
Portland Traction Co., 182, 194
Portland, Vancouver & Yakima Railroad Co., 248
Portland Zoological Gardens, 255
Portland Zoo Railway, 255
Portsmouth, Oregon, 178
Powers, Oregon, 137
Prairie City, Oregon, 91, 92, 94
Prineville, Oregon, 100, 128, 129
Prodfitt, Vern, 14
Proffitt, James, 10
Promised Land, 199
Purdon, Clarence, 36

— Q —
Quakers, 241

— R —
Ray's Landing, 4, 5, 20, 65, 70, 133
Reedsport, Oregon, 138, 140
Red Bluff, California, 29
Red Electric Circle Trip, 239
Red Electrics, 40, 79, 156, 230, 231, 232, 233, 234, 235, 236, 237, 238, 239, 240, 241, 242, 243, 245, 246, 247
Redmond, Oregon, 125, 128
Reedsville, Oregon, 108
Reid, William, 67
Reith, Oregon, 97
Reno, Nevada, 91, 146
Rice, Ella, 14
Rivera, Oregon, 79
Riverdale, Oregon, 79, 243, 244
Road of a Thousand Wonders, 72
Rockaway, Oregon, 109, 111
Rocky Butte, Oregon, 48
Rocky Mountains, 17
Rogue River Valley, 37, 132
Rogue River Valley Railway Co., 169, 170, 171, 172
Rohse, Bert, 237
Roland, Shirley E., 40, 41
Roseburg, Oregon, 13, 17, 32, 43, 142
Russian Decapods, 257, 258, 259

– S –

Sacramento, California, 29
St. Charles Hotel, 226
St. Helens, Oregon, 7
St. Johns Motor Line, 178
St. Johns, Oregon, 178, 223
St. Joseph, Oregon, 13, 39, 40, 231
St. Mary's Church, 71
St. Paul, Minnesota, 63, 77
St. Paul, Oregon, 5, 20, 65, 70
Salem Falls City & Western Railway Co., 163, 164, 165, 166, 167, 168
Salem Hotel, 208
Salem, Oregon, 9, 22, 23, 25, 28, 70, 133, 134, 148, 163, 164, 165, 168, 195, 201, 205, 208, 214, 222, 225
Salmonberry, Oregon, 109
Sandy River, 48
San Francisco, California, 23, 27, 33, 37, 75, 82, 86, 120, 130, 148, 233
Santiam Canyon, 84, 222
Santiam River, 89
Scappoose Bay, 249
Scappoose, Oregon, 122
Scio, Oregon, 75, 76, 133
Sconlon, Sam, 80
Scott, Charles Napier, 4, 6
Seashore Road Co., 118
Seaside, Oregon, 106, 115, 116, 118, 120
Seattle, Washington, 64, 104, 115
Sellwood Bridge, 78
Seneca, Oregon, 99
Settlemier, Jess, 20
Shaniko, Oregon, 100, 101
Shasta Daylight, 23
Shasta Limited, 21
Shasta Route, 145
Sheridan, Oregon, 4, 65, 69, 78, 156, 242
Sheridan & Willamina Railway Co., 156, 157
Sherman Anti-Trust Act, 96
Silver Falls, Timber Co., 195
Silver Lake, Oregon, 162
Silverton, Oregon, 3, 4, 20, 65, 70, 71, 75, 133, 195
Siskiyou County, 250
Siskiyou Line, 142, 145
Siskiyou, Oregon, 33
Skinner, W. W., 25
Slingerland, Geo., 10
Smith, Frank M., 10
Smith, Walter L., 160
Snake River, 44
Southern Oregon Traction Co., 169, 171
Southern Pacific Company, V, IX, 6, 13, 14, 16, 20, 29, 65, 70, 73, 75, 77, 85, 88, 96, 106, 112, 120, 129, 133, 134, 136, 138, 141,

142, 146, 148, 150, 154, 158, 159, 161, 163, 165, 166, 168, 177, 187, 195, 222, 225, 228, 230, 231, 232, 233, 234, 235, 236, 237, 239, 240, 242, 244, 247, 250, 251, 252, 253
Spangler, Oregon, 197
Spaulding, Charles K., 163
Sperle, Eugene, F., 72
Spokane, Portland & Seattle Railroad Co., 10, 119, 124, 125, 216, 218
Spooner, Floyd Jasper, 81
Springfield, Oregon, 30, 73
Stanfield, Oregon, 53
Stanton Street Station, 178
Stark Street Ferry, 179, 181
Steel Bridge, 14, 47, 178
Sterling, Paul, 40
Steward, Gordon, 91
Strahorn, Robert E., 161
Street Cars (Electric): Albany—226, 227; Astoria—225; Eugene—228; Forest Grove—224; Portland—223; Salem—225
Street Cars (Horse Drawn): Albany—226; Astoria—224; Baker—229; Corvallis—228; Klamath Falls (Linkville)—229; Portland—222
Stump Dodger, 91
Sullivan's Gulch, 47
Summit, Oregon (Benton County), 87
Summit, Oregon (Harney County), 99
Sumpter, Oregon, 91, 94
Sumpter, Valley Railway Co., V, 91, 92, 93, 95
Susanville, Oregon, 91

– T –

Tacoma Ferry, 64
Tacoma, Washington, 7, 64, 104, 115
Talent, Oregon, 31
Tallman, Oregon, 133
Taylor, William, 36
Telocaset, Oregon, 96
Texas, The, 155
The Cascades, 82
"The Country Boy," 73
The Dalles, Oregon, 52, 103, 146
Thomas, Cliff, 37
Thomas, Oregon, 89
Thompson, John Mrs., 18
Thrall, California, 249, 250, 251
Three Sisters, 82
Tillamook Bay, 114
Tillamook Burn, 109
Tillamook County, 108, 110, 112, 256
Tillamook, Oregon, 106, 107, 109, 111, 112, 252

Tillamook Gate, Oregon, 252
Timber, Oregon, 108
T. J. Potter, Steamboat, 98
Tipton, Oregon, 93
Toledo, Oregon, 84, 85
Troutdale, Oregon, 48, 185, 190, 191, 193
Tualatin Plains, 5
Tualatin River, 246, 247
Tunnel No. 13, 33, 34
Turner, Oregon, 26

– U –

Umatilla, Oregon, 55, 57
Umatilla Central Railroad Co., 97
Umatilla County, 55, 63
Umatilla River, 55
Union Pacific Railroad, 44, 45, 47, 48, 60, 62, 96, 97, 100, 104, 105, 106, 123, 161
Union Station, Portland, 7, 8, 9, 10, 14, 47, 79, 134, 230, 237
United Brethren Church, 86
Union Cove & Valley Railway, 60
United Railways Co., 202, 216, 217, 218, 219
Union County, 60
Union Junction, 60
Union, Oregon, 60
Union Railroad, 60
Union Street & Suburban Railway, 60
University of Oregon, 29
University Park, Oregon, 178
U.S. Government, 86

– V –

Vale, Oregon, 96
Valley & Siletz Railroad Co., 172, 173, 174, 175, 176, 177
Valsetz, Oregon, 172, 174, 176, 177
Van Brunt, Henry, 9
Vancouver Ferry, 179, 180
Vancouver, Washington, 179, 181, 248
Vernonia, Oregon, 218
Vetter, Harry, 70
Village Green, Oregon, 153
Villard, Henry, 9, 13, 32, 39, 43, 44, 47, 57, 69, 70, 133
Vulcan Iron Works, 75

– W –

Wald, Anna, 27
Walla Walla & Columbia River Railroad Co., 43
Walla Walla Valley Railway Co., 220
Walla Walla Valley Traction Co., 220
Walla Walla, Washington, 220
Wallowa County, 60
Wallowa Lake State Park & Mountains, 60, 96

Wallowa, Oregon, 61
Wallula, Washington, 43, 44, 47
Warren, Oregon, 121
Warrenton, Oregon, 115
Wasco County, 103
Wasco, Oregon, 101, 102
Washington & Columbia River Railroad, 63
Waters Creek, Oregon, 143, 147
Weathers, Ray, 81
Weed, California, 142
Wegner, Alida, 154
Welch, Alvadore, 148, 222, 225
Wells Fargo, 88
West Linn, Oregon, 148, 222, 246, 247
Western Oregon Railroad Co., 39, 40, 78
Western Pacific Railroad, 129
Westfir, Oregon, 145
West Salem, Oregon, 163, 165, 167
West Scio, Oregon, 75, 76
West Side Line, 13, 28
"West Side Local," 234, 236
West Stayton, Oregon, 73, 74, 75
West Woodburn, Oregon, 207
Wheeler Lumber Co., 108, 113
Wheeler, Oregon, 113
Whiteson, Oregon (White's), 40, 78, 156, 242, 243

Wilkesboro, Oregon, 202, 216, 217, 221
Willamette Bridge Railway Co., 178
Willamette Industries, 163
Willamette, Oregon, 246, 247
Willamette Pacific Railroad Co., 141
Willamette River, 4, 7, 9, 13, 14, 20, 43, 44, 47, 65, 70, 78, 79, 133, 134, 163, 164, 179, 187, 199, 237
Willamette Slough, 122
Willamette Transportation Locks Co., 43
Willamette Valley, 11, 21, 26, 44, 65, 77, 82, 133, 199, 204, 207, 208, 230
Willamette Valley & Coast Railroad Co., 253
Willamette Valley Chautauqua Assn., 16
Willamette Valley Lumber Co., 163
Willamette Valley Railway, 195
Willamette Valley Route, 199
Willamette Valley Southern Railway Co., 195, 196, 197, 198
Willamina & Grand Ronde Railway, 97, 154, 157

Willamina, Oregon, 65, 154, 156
Willapa Bay, Washington, 98
Willett, Si, 240
Willow Creek, 62
Willsburg Junction, Oregon, 134, 135
Willson, Wm. Holden, 208
Wilson, Lillie, 89
Wishram, Washington, 130
Woodburn, Oregon, 3, 4, 20, 65, 70, 73, 133, 144, 207
Woodlawn, Oregon, 179
Woods, Geo., 85
Woods, Geo. L., 11

— Y —
Yacolt, Oregon, 248
Yakima, Oregon, 248
Yamhill, Oregon, 232
Yamhill River, 13, 65, 78
Yaquina Bay, 82, 84, 86
Yaquina, Oregon, 82, 84, 85, 88
Yaquina Route, 82
Yaquina, Steamer, 84
Yosemite Valley, 233
Young's Bay, 118
Young, Wood, 18

— Z —
"Zooliners," 255